Foul Deeds and Suspic...

OXFORDSHIRE

CARL BOARDMAN

Series Editor
Brian Elliott

Wharncliffe Books

First Published in 2004 by
Wharncliffe Books
an imprint of
Pen and Sword Books Limited,
47 Church Street, Barnsley,
South Yorkshire. S70 2AS

*For up-to-date information on other titles produced under the
Wharncliffe imprint, please telephone or write to:*

Wharncliffe Books
FREEPOST
47 Church Street
Barnsley
South Yorkshire S70 2BR
Telephone (24 hours): 01226 - 734555

ISBN: 1–903425–56–5

For a complete list of Wharncliffe titles, please contact
Wharncliffe Books Limited
47 Church Street, Barnsley, South Yorkshire, S70 2AS, England
E-mail: enquiries@pen-and-sword.co.uk
Website: www.pen-and-sword.co.uk

A CIP catalogue record of this book is available from the
British Library

Printed in the United Kingdom by
CPI UK

Contents

Introduction

I n the roadway of Broad Street in Oxford, just outside what was Blackwell's Children's Bookshop and is now a rather superior lingerie emporium, a large metal cross is set into the tarmac. It marks the spot where three men were burned to death for failing to move with the prevailing wind of religious conformity. Walk down past Waterstone's Bookshop, along by the New Theatre, and turn left towards Gloucester Green market square, and on the modern wall of a laser game provider is a plaque commemorating a group of Civil War soldiers who made the mistake of believing that the end of monarchy meant the coming of equality, and were shot by their own side – using something a lot more old fashioned than lasers, but just as deadly.

Thirty seconds' walk due north brings you to Beaumont Street, where a group of students were attacked, and one of them killed, by a set of townsmen who took the Town versus Gown quarrels seriously. The same street along which the Oxfordshire Yeomanry galloped trying to escape from a mob flinging rocks at their heads while rescuing a gang of agricultural rioters.

Past and present are very close in Oxford and its surrounding county, and sometimes they seem to merge. There are plenty of byways in the city where only a wavy set of double yellow lines reminds you that you aren't in the nineteenth century, or the seventeenth, or perhaps even the fourteenth.... You wouldn't be entirely surprised to stumble over the body of a dying prostitute, or meet the notorious highwayman Captain James Hind in one of the low-ceilinged, oak-beamed pubs which have survived since long before he rode the lonely lanes of Oxfordshire.

Or perhaps it particularly feels that way if you spend your working life in the Oxfordshire Record Office, where the records of these and many other stories of the county are stored. Some of the stories have turned into legends, and gained a gloss of inaccuracies over the years, but one of the advantages of being an archivist is that you have the chance to

A View of the City of Oxford.

Prospect of Oxford by the seventeenth-century engraver Loggan.

go back to the original sources and find out what really happened. Of course that isn't a prerogative confined to the professionals, and perhaps more people should take advantage of it. But until you do, this handy little compendium introduces you to some of the more notorious individuals in Oxfordshire's past, ruthless in their pursuit of money or power, or sometimes just too stupid to see that their selfishness was going to leave their tracks strewn with corpses.

Most of the stories and illustrations come from the collections in Oxfordshire Record Office, though the items relating to Brasenose College come courtesy of my wife, Elizabeth Boardman, who is College Archivist. And I owe a special thanks to Mrs Jenny Higgins of Kidlington, who provided not only the story of the Dunsdon highwaymen – her own ancestors – but also the pictures of the tree from which they were hung in chains.

For those wanting to delve in greater detail, a handful of the stories have been exhaustively researched from sources within the Record Office and elsewhere. Those interested in Giles Covington should see *The Abingdon Waterturnpike Murder* by Mark Davies, published just as this work was going to press, while more stories of James Hind will be found in *The*

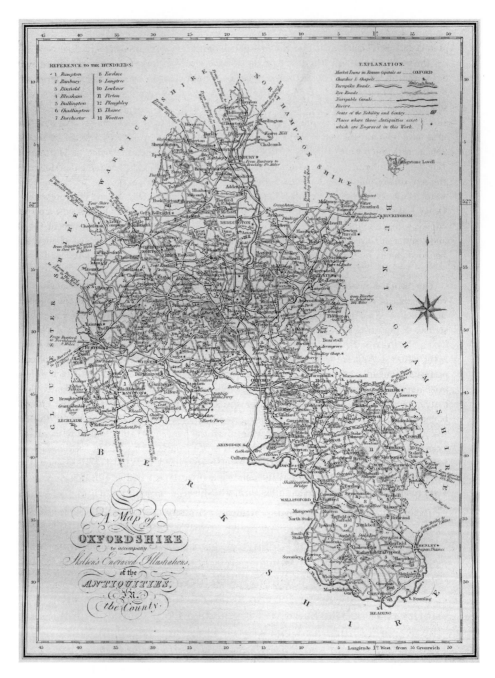

Skelton's map of the county of Oxfordshire.

Adventures of Captain James Hind of Chipping Norton: the Oxfordshire Highwayman by O M Meades, and further detail on the Kalabergo affair in *John Kalabergo of Banbury* by E R Lester. But most of the stories have never seen print outside an old broadsheet or yellowing newspaper, often not even that. I cannot, however, resist adding that for those who still have an appetite for the misdeeds of their fellows at the end of this book, there are more of them in my *Oxfordshire Sinners and Villains*, available through the Oxfordshire Record Office.

For now, however, take a deep breath and prepare for murder, accident, arson, judicial slaughter, flesh-eating creatures, and even a sporting event which went horribly wrong. There's a lot more to Oxford than punting gently down the Cherwell, and even Alice found that what started as a lazy picnic ended with someone screaming, 'Off with her head!' Nobody moved. Lucky Alice; in real-life Oxfordshire she'd have been trampled in the rush.

CHAPTER 1

Shadrach Smith – The Robber Gypsy 1762

Many of our prejudices are fuelled by misunderstood history. Running away with the gypsies, stolen by the gypsies – the primaeval fear emerges of those who don't work to the same rules as the rest of society, who have always been different and refused to fit in. When a scapegoat is needed they are ready to hand, and if we continue to fear or suspect them we also conveniently forget that they were victims. Everyone knows of the fate of the Jews in Nazi Germany; the similar fate of the gypsies is less well known.

England, with its dislike of sturdy beggars and vagrants, was quick to pass laws against them; an act was made against their itinerancy in 1530, and in the reign of Charles I thirteen people were executed at one assizes for having associated with them. By contrast, their attempts to settle down roused equal resentment, and their settlement at Norwood was broken up in 1797.

It was not surprising, therefore, that the crimes of Shadrach Smith aroused considerable interest and condemnation from the broadsheet writers of the eighteenth century. Smith was actually born at the Norwood settlement in the early years of the century, and was related to Mary Squires, who was involved in one of the most famous court cases of the era; she was accused of robbing and kidnapping Elizabeth Canning, and was only pardoned when evidence emerged that Canning's testimony may have been perjured. It was claimed that Smith had given legal advice to Squires in the case, as he'd spent so much time dodging a series of charges brought against him that he knew more about the loopholes in the law than many attorneys.

Smith's official employment was catching polecats and destroying vermin; while he was doing this, his sons spent their time pilfering around the neighbourhood, and his wife and daughters hawked various trifles around from door to door. This not only gave them the opportunity of picking the pockets of those who asked to have their fortunes told, but also enabled them to spy out the lie of the land in various houses; where the poultry was kept, whether the householders were careful about security and so forth. It was low-key villainy, but Shadrach was soon to carry it onto another plane.

On 22 March 1762, near Chalgrove Field, he lay in wait for some unsuspecting victim; knowing that the farm labourers had received their wages, it seemed an appropriate time to transfer the cash to his own pocket. In fact it seemed his luck was in; it was a lone girl who came down the lane, but one who was determined to hang on to what she had:

He stopped her and with shocking threats and imprecations demanded her money, and the poor creature being very unwilling to lose it, though the sum she was possessed of was very small, he threw her down in the ditch, in part stripped her, and with his knees upon her body used her with such violence that the blood gushed from her mouth and nose.

A contemporary woodcut – Smith's victim is discovered, while he swings from a rope in the background.

Evidently Smith was quite willing to kill his victim, but one of his sons was more squeamish. This was not the usual MO of the family; petty theft and swindling were more in their line, and the boy didn't want to be involved in this level of violence. He begged his father to stop and show mercy to the girl; this only made Smith more determined, and eventually when his son persisted he left the girl and went for him instead, so that the boy had to run and hide himself in a corn field. But Smith had gone too far; the son denounced his father to the authorities, and Smith was brought to trial at Oxford.

Evidently there was only one tender-hearted member of the Smith family, as the rest of its members sided with Shadrach. After the son had given evidence, they tracked him down and forced him to return to court and swear that everything he had said was a tissue of lies, occasioned by money and promises offered him by the prosecution. 'There may be just cause to dread what will be the boy's fate from the exasperated and abandoned gang,' said the commentator, 'for having given testimony against his father.' But all the claims of perjury were no help to Shadrach, who was sentenced to hang.

Even then, he found an odd sort of consolation. 'He comforted himself,' the broadsheet of his execution stated, 'with having lived longer in the world than many others of his own fraternity, who thought themselves more lucky for escaping the gallows.' And indeed he was almost sixty, not a bad age for a travelling man in those days. His final words on the scaffold were a warning to all parents not to put their lives in the hands of their children. But by then he was already going into folklore as one more sinister gypsy to boost the stereotype; the scruples of his son were much sooner forgotten.

Shadrach Smith hangs from the gallows.

CHAPTER 2

The Ascott Women –
The Sex War Reaches the Unions
1873

T he Tolpuddle Martyrs had been convicted and sentenced in 1834 for administering an illegal oath; their case was one of the crucial stages in the formation of the trades union movement in Britain. In 1871 the Liberal government finally legalized unions and their activities – except one. Although unions had the right to exist and the right to strike, they didn't have the right to picket. It remained illegal to prevent anyone else from going to work.

This, of course, put a serious spoke in the wheel of unions achieving anything in times of economic depression and serious unemployment; there would always be someone willing to take the jobs that the unionized workers refused to do. The fact was brought home in no uncertain terms to the men employed by Robert Hambidge, tenant of Crown Farm

The village of Ascott-under-Wychwood as seen on the nineteenth-century tithe.

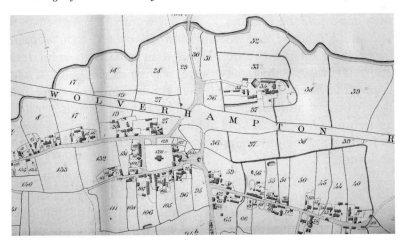

in Ascott-under-Wychwood. Hambidge's men had joined Joseph Arch's new National Agricultural Labourers' Union, formed to combat the appallingly low wages of farmhands, and tried out their new power in April 1873 by demanding a rise in pay from 10 shillings to 14 shillings a week. Hambidge refused. The men went on strike, and for a while did rather worse than their employer; they had to struggle along on what the union could afford to give them, while Hambidge thanked his lucky stars that they'd chosen to confront him at the one time of year when there wasn't much work to do. But as summer drew on, the tables began to turn.

Desperate to keep his farm afloat, Hambidge went out and hired fresh labour – to be exact, two boys of about eighteen from Ramsden by the names of John Hodgkins and John Millin, whom he put up in the farmhouse. On 12 May he went off to Stow Fair, telling the two lads to get on with hoeing the turnip field. But when they arrived at the field gate they found a reception committee – a group of some thirty or forty individuals, a number of whom were armed with sticks, determined to stop the lads getting to their work. What amazed Hodgkins and Millin was that it wasn't the angry farm labourers. It was a group of women.

The unionized workers themselves were sticking to the rules; if they started picketing the National Agricultural Labourers' Union would disown them and withdraw their only means of support. But that didn't apply to their wives, their mothers, their sisters.... All the womenfolk had turned up, and Hodgkins and Millin soon discovered that women could be a lot more intimidating than men with a lot less effort. It wasn't that they were waving their hefty sticks around. It was more that they were threatening to remove the lads' trousers, and while being beaten with sticks didn't much appeal, for an eighteen year old having your trousers removed in front of a gang of laughing women was humiliation beyond endurance.

When the women suggested going home for a drink to discuss matters, somehow it sounded a bit different than if a group of good, honest men had suggested it, and the lads screamed for the police. The women turned seriously threatening, and threw one of the boys over a stile. The single village constable who was available managed to note down seventeen names from the crowd before the rest of them melted away to their cottages, and as far as he was concerned he'd met intimidation with intimidation and that was the end of the matter. But when Robert Hambidge arrived home and found his turnips unhoed he lost his temper and took out a private prosecution against the women.

Or at least that was what Hambidge's prosecution claimed happened. The women had another story. For a start, they claimed that only one of them had a stick, and that was a little girl who'd taken it from a carpenter passing by and was playing with it. They said the lads had seen the justice of their case when they explained it and said they'd collect the wages they were owed and go, rather than take bread out of other men's mouths – it was Hambidge who forced them back to work. They didn't call the constable; that was Hambidge's wife. And as for the stile incident, one of the lads was playing with some of the younger girls and fell, but he laughed about it louder than anyone.

It was at the trial that things started to get out of hand. The magistrates who tried the case at Chadlington Sessions were the Reverend Thomas Harris of Swerford and the Reverend William Carter of Sarsden – both respectable clergymen of the Church of England. Unfortunately at least half the seventeen women were nonconformists, and it looked like a few private scores were being settled. On top of this, Joseph Arch had seen how he might make political capital out of the affair. If the women went to gaol there would be a public outcry – he could see to that – so it might be useful to ensure that Ascott got some martyrs to compare with Tolpuddle. He ensured that the women had no legal representation in court.

When it came down to it, it was the word of two eighteen-year-old lads against that of seventeen women whose honesty had never been questioned before. Realistically, whatever had happened, there was no way the court could find against the women. Harris and Carter found a way; they simply ignored everything the women said, believed the boys implicitly, and proceeded to judgement. To do Carter justice, he did ask

10 Saint James' Square,
10 June 1873.

My Lord

In reply to your Lordship's
Letter of the 4th instant I have the
honour to inform you that having
communicated the contents of the
Letter to the Reverend Mr Harris
and the Reverend Mr Carter, and
invited them to furnish me with their
own explanation of the recent judgment
which has been impugned, they have
favoured me with the Answers which I
beg to transmit to your Lordship.

It is very satisfactory to know
that, – as expressed by your Lordship's
Letter, – the evidence given before the
Magistrates sufficiently proved the
Offence with which the sixteen Women
were charged, and that the Offence was
one with which it was right and proper
for the Magistrates to deal seriously."

And I beg permission to submit, as
my own view of the Law, that, inasmuch
as the Magistrates by their sentence
kept abundantly within the Law they
were administering, they were entitled, –

The letter from the Duke of Marlborough, insisting that the magistrates' punishment of the Ascott Women was perfectly justified.

Hambidge to withdraw the prosecution, but the farmer absolutely refused.

Astonishingly one of the women was acquitted, but the other sixteen got from seven to ten days hard labour. Waves of shock spread around the neighbourhood – a similar case at Woodstock a few months earlier had resulted in the men involved being released on their own recognizances. This was the heaviest penalty the magistrates could impose. The sixteen prisoners were placed in the cells in Chipping Norton police station to await transportation to the women's wing of Oxford Prison. Before the transport could be arranged, a mob of 2,000 angry locals had formed in the street outside, and the police station was under attack.

By nine in the evening the whole area in front of the police station in Rock Hill was crowded, and numbers were swelling all the time. Some were curious locals, come to see what all the fuss was about; some were genuine supporters of the Union and sympathizers with the women; but many were the local toughs out for violence. Superintendent Lakin took one look, locked the door, and sent an urgent message to Oxford for assistance. Cries went up to free the women, mixed with slogans of support for the Union, and, as the *Oxford Journal* tactfully put it, 'Mr Hambidge was not forgotten'. Then the cries became uglier: free the women or we tear down the station and fetch them ourselves. At this point the first stone was thrown.

Chipping Norton, scene of the riot outside the police station.

Lakin heard the breaking of glass and went down on to the path, where he saw William Barry, a local mason, holding a large rock. He called out, but Barry flung it at the light in the guard room passage, shattering the whole thing; he shouted, 'Barry, I saw you do that!' but then another man started throwing stones and he dodged back inside. Edward Belcher took it one stage further; he flung a stone through the window of Lakin's house, smashing the shutters – Lakin found it in the middle of his carpet. Members of the crowd were drinking and getting wilder; William Hewer was flourishing a big stick and yelling, 'Come on, lads, stick to the Union. Fetch out the women.'

At about ten, the Mayor arrived to quieten the mob, but no one listened to him. Slates were now being torn off the roof. The police decided to sit it out – the station was solidly built, and the crowd would get bored if nothing happened. Besides, help was coming from Oxford – wasn't it? Gradually the disturbance wound down. By midnight, the mob was dispersing. At one in the morning the police were quite relaxed when the reinforcements from Oxford came galloping round the corner into a near-empty street.

Still, that gave them the chance to hurry the women out, into a heavy wagon, and off to the gaol. They'd got through the tricky bit – from now on, they reckoned, it would be all plain sailing. They couldn't have been more wrong.

News of the riot trickled up to London, and the nationals pricked up their ears. Reporters started to flood into the county to investigate the story, and what they found had the makings of a first-class scandal. Delicate women – all right, they were the wives of labourers but you could stretch a point – condemned by a couple of pompous clerics and sent to do hard labour for trying to keep the bread in their children's mouths. 'Impossible', thundered the headline in *The Times*. Editorials supported the women, and roundly condemned everyone else in the case.

The *Daily News* showed an instinct for playing on public emotion which would be the envy of today's tabloids:

> *The humble cottagers in Ascott are much shocked by the callous indifference displayed by their well-to-do neighbours as to the welfare of the children left for the time motherless. A little orphan was pointed out to me this afternoon whose only relative, an aunt, was taken to prison. Not an enquiry was made about the child by the so-called well-to-do classes.*

Meanwhile they got their knife well into Hambidge, whose farm was 'much too large' and who 'owns an immense slice of the parish'.

The debate reached the highest in the land. Queen Victoria expressed her support for the women, though there might have been a hidden agenda here; she detested Gladstone, whose Government was seen as being responsible for a law under which this could happen. Indeed she demanded their immediate release, and a frantic correspondence was set up between the Home Secretary and the Duke of Marlborough, Lord Lieutenant of Oxfordshire. Marlborough hated the Union, and staunchly upheld both the verdict and the punishment, claiming that such combinations were 'to the injury alike of private and public interests' – the private interests, of course being those of the wealthy, who were the only ones who mattered. Similarly he sent along a testimonial from the inhabitants of the area around Ascott, supporting the verdict, but it was notable that these inhabitants were the ones whose interest was in keeping wages down.

Meanwhile another emotive problem had arisen: Mary and Elizabeth Pratley both had babies with them, and claims were being made that the infants were suffering in the prison. The authorities went out of their way to investigate, and found that *each child was supplied every morning and every evening with a full half pint of new milk and also with six ounces of bread each day, as usually allowed for babies. In addition, the prison matron made some sop with sugar for Elizabeth Pratley's child every day, as she said her child had been accustomed to have sugar.*

The women, they said, had made no complaint. This may have been true while they were inside; however, once out of the prison walls an independent witness interviewed them and heard quite a different story.

Mary Pratley, whose baby was ten weeks old, said

I had as good a breast of milk as any woman in England when I went into prison, but while there had scarcely any, owing to my not having proper food. I got rheumatism in my shoulders and limbs very bad owing to the night drive which was both cold and wet. My baby was taken away undressed from Chipping Norton police station in the middle of the night. I begged Superintendent Lakin to give me time to put the child's clothes on, but he refused, saying, 'You must come at once, there is no time to mess about.' The child took a very bad cough, and coughed till it was black in the face on the Sunday. The doctor made no enquiry as to my state or that of the baby.

At the same time, Elizabeth Pratley had similar worries about her child:

I received for it what they called a pint but was no more than three quarters of a pint of milk. The child suffered very much for want of proper nourishment and from there being no fire in the cell. It could not sleep at night it was so hungry.

The reigning monarch was not to be denied, and it was decided that the magistrates had been a little over-zealous. The women were given a free and complete pardon, and the order was sent out for their release. Unfortunately the wheels of bureaucracy moved so slowly that this did not come through until ten days after the start of their sentence – the day they were due to be released anyway. Still, their release was

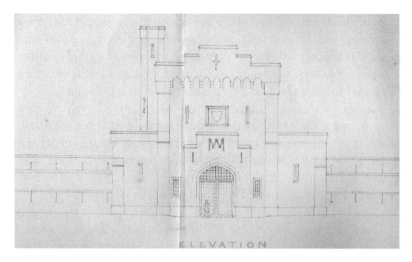

Oxford Gaol, where the women spent their imprisonment ...

accompanied by the gift of red flannel petticoats from the
Queen, not something many inmates of Oxford Gaol can
claim to have received.

The women were feted on their release; they were cheered
by a crowd of 150 outside the prison, given a hearty breakfast,
and taken to the King's Arms in Woodstock for lunch. After
lunch Mr Holloway, secretary of the Union, made a point of

... and the plan of the wing in which they were held.

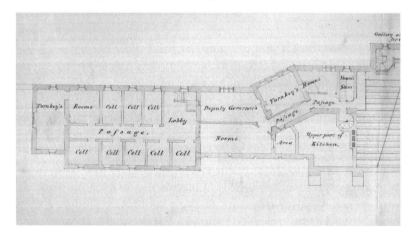

taking them into Blenheim Park and past the Duke of Marlborough's front door, just to rub it in. Then they travelled on to Chipping Norton to be reunited with their families, where a crowd of some 2,000 greeted them, in a less violent mood than the one ten days earlier.

On the surface it looked like the women had achieved very little, but that was deceptive. Harris and Carter had sealed the death warrant of clergymen acting as magistrates; very quietly over the next few years the number of clergymen on the bench was run down. The Liberal government fell shortly afterwards, and Disraeli's new administration made a point of changing the law relating to picketing. And finally the men did get their pay rise. A pity that it was followed by a massive agricultural depression which made it largely irrelevant. Real life can be very unfair.

Warrant to the local Constable to take the women to imprisonment in Oxford Gaol.

CHAPTER 3

The Black Rat – Fun in Charlbury and Shorthampton 1609

About ten days after Whitsunday 1609, a certain John Charles, churchwarden of Shorthampton, ran across one of his neighbours, Nicholas Harris, as they were walking down to the wood there. Harris vaguely recalled his wife telling him that Charles had been making dark comments about the curate of Shorthampton, William Forrest, and asked what it was all about.

I'll tell you, said Charles. I was on my way home on Whit Monday, just coming down by Bickstone Bottom, when I heard this great heaving, blowing and groaning in the bushes. I thought someone was stealing a deer, or maybe some great beast had fallen down and couldn't get up again, but when I took a look it was the curate, lying on top of Clemence Beckingham with his hose undone, getting his leg over her.

And thus began the unravelling of the dubious activities of Shorthampton. Forrest and Clemence were unlucky; anyone else and they might have got away with it, but Charles took his duties as churchwarden seriously. 'An honest, plain man and very careful in that he undertaketh', they called him; more to the point he had been elected churchwarden the previous Easter, and so was relatively new in the exercise of his powers. And now he'd found the local cleric in *flagrante dilecto* – how could he resist? The trouble was, he didn't realize what a hornets' nest he'd opened.

Jurisdiction in the mediaeval period had been very complex; a

The Black Rat would have recognized this bit of medieval Charlbury, which lasted until the twentieth century.

network of courts and authorities. In an era of slow travel and limited communications our modern notions of centralized justice were simply impossible. Local notables had power in particular areas; the court of Quarter Sessions emerged in which local justices could deal with misdemeanours, while individual manorial lordships had authority over local customs and sometimes overlapped with the Sessions. For serious, capital crimes royal justices were sent from London to hold the Assizes, and those accused of serious wrongdoing might find themselves in gaol for months, waiting for the royal officials to reach them.

In the midst of all this stood the church. A powerful institution with its own equivalent of nobility in the bishops, it expected and got special treatment. The bishop and archdeacon of any diocese could hold a court to deal with offences committed by their clergy; they also expected to be allowed to deal with any cases specifically concerned with offences against the law of God which were not covered in the conventional courts – which basically came down to moral issues. As the mediaeval period turned into the early modern, the rights of the church were toned down; a murderous clergyman was not going to get off by appealing to his fellow churchmen, and might well simply be handed over to the secular arm. But for minor crimes concerning the clergy, and for anything to do with the morality of clergy or laity, the Church Courts still stood – their concentration on moral matters earning them the nickname of the Bawdy Courts.

It was before this court that Charles determined to take Forrest. When word got back to Clemence Beckingham that Charles was accusing them, she went to ask him if he'd really seen her and Forrest; when he replied he had she said, 'Then we are undone.' But if Charles thought he was the first person to reveal the dubious side of the curate's character, he was soon to discover that he'd been living in the dark for years. The first thing he learned was that half the parish seemed to be referring to Forrest as the Black Rat. Several people cheerfully recounted the story of ten years ago, when one William Locke came to the house of Thomas Margettes of Shorthampton to find only his wife at home. While they were talking, he heard a great rattling sound coming from upstairs, and when he asked Margettes' wife what on earth it was, she said, 'Oh, we've got terrible problems with rats.' Reckoning that any rat capable of making that noise was likely to be eating the house next, Locke ran upstairs to find out what was going on, and discovered the curate naked with one Cicely Franklin. Interesting rat, he observed, and the nickname stuck. But that was only the beginning. Richard Coates was cited as one who wouldn't let the curate in his house, because he suspected him of having an affair with his wife. Forrest was said to have beaten up a certain Ralffe House and then had sex with his wife on the stairs; when House heard his bed rattling he went up to see what was going on and found them hard at it. Anne Cottrell was one woman the curate didn't sleep with, but it wasn't for want of trying; he offered her a waistcoat as a bribe to get her into bed. Anne Churchley and Barbara Cotterell were named as two more of his intended victims. One is left wondering if Forrest had any free time or energy left for his work in the church.

Witnesses explain how the Black Rat got his name.

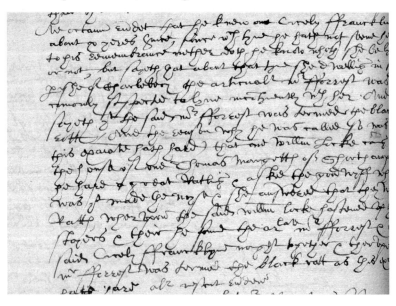

Did no one stand up for him? Well yes, one Robert Maunder said that he believed Forrest behaved honestly in his calling, and that Clemence was an honest woman. He would, though, wouldn't he, said several other witnesses, seeing as how he's been sleeping with her whenever Forrest was off after someone else. Maunder had been blind since the previous summer, but that hadn't stopped him; now, instead of making his own way to her house he had to get someone to lead him, which wasn't the best way of keeping an affair quiet. Clemence at least tried to cover up their activities; she kept a cow at Maunder's house and went there regularly to milk it, at which times Maunder did 'tooth her rakes' – which those in the parish commonly believed meant illicit sex.

All of which went to show how unwise it could be to lift up rocks in the average parish and see what crawled out from beneath. It was quite obvious from the various witnesses that everyone knew what sort of a man Forrest was and what he got up to, but no one was going to start slinging mud in case some of it got slung back – right until John Charles literally stumbled over Forrest and got officious. Forrest ended up being censured in the courts, but that didn't mean Charlbury got rid of him. One is left to wonder just what life was like for the village inhabitants after all their little secrets had been dragged out into the open.

CHAPTER 4

The Shipton Railway Disaster –
Never Trust Your Friends
1874

Oxfordshire's worst ever railway disaster was also the Great Western's worst; something so simple, so easily avoided, which nevertheless resulted in enormous loss of life. Yet the irony was that not only were the flaws shown up in one of the country's most respected railway companies. All the way down the line, those involved showed a degree of greed and stupidity which must have made the passengers wonder if they had been singled out like Job for their own personal nightmare.

Starting as it meant to go on, the tragedy took place on the most emotionally sensitive day of the year – Christmas Eve. The year was 1874, when at the start of a bitter winter the

Thirty years after the crash, Shipton was trying to sell itself as a quiet little village – but no one had forgotten.

The point at which the crash took place, showing why the Paper Mill was the obvious place to take the injured.

holidays put immense pressure on the railways as people travelled to be with their families over the holiday. The Paddington to Birkenhead train was pulling fourteen packed coaches, and when it arrived at Oxford station half an hour late – at least some things don't change – there was no room for any of the waiting passengers to board.

If the train had gone on without them, those waiting at Oxford would doubtless have been extremely angry and written to the company, if not *The Times*. In fact it would have been the luckiest escape of their lives. Instead, the Great Western decided to add an extra coach just behind the engine to accommodate them. Unfortunately they were short of rolling stock, and put on an ancient little four-wheeler, completely at odds with the rest of the carriages. And the little four-wheeler was carrying a sinister secret which was to cause considerable embarrassment to Great Western.

Its tyres were fixed to the wheels by four countersunk rivets through the rims. Decades ago this had been seen as a dangerous method of attachment; as early as 1855 the company had decided to discontinue using countersunk rivets in this way. Oddly enough, the coach had been built in that very year, but for the Newport, Abergavenny and Hereford Railway. Were Great Western paying the price for using rolling stock from a less fastidious company? Well, not exactly; in 1868, six years before the disaster, they had replaced the tyres using just the same outmoded method.

Meanwhile the Oxford stationmaster, Gibbs, had been advised that the engine would never get a string of what was now fifteen carriages over Hatton Bank, just north of Leamington, and he agreed to add a second engine to assist. In this innocent way he increased the power of the train and ensured that when the accident happened it had a lot of momentum behind it. Then the train pulled out of Oxford station and off towards Kidlington.

By the time it passed through Woodstock station it was doing forty miles an hour and going well. It wasn't until it was approaching the bridge over the Cherwell that the front, right-hand wheel of the ancient coach began to disintegrate. A piece of the tyre flew off, and instantly the coach became unsteady, held upright only by the tension with the engine pulling it.

The passengers knew what had gone wrong – or at least that something had. They had to stop the train, and fortunately there was a way of doing so: the communication cord. They tugged it. Absolutely nothing happened.

The first the engine driver, Richard, knew about it was when he turned round on his footplate and saw a cascade of snow and debris flying up from the damaged coach. While he was trying to work out what was happening, his fireman saw a man hanging out of the coach window frantically waving his arms and yelling 'Whoa! Whoa!'. His eye immediately went to the alarm gong which should have been activated by the communication cord. The clapper was moving in a slow, lazy fashion, without anything like enough speed to sound the gong. At the subsequent enquiry there was an attempt to fix blame on the man who connected up the cord, but it was a non-starter. Everyone knew the Harrison communication cord was hopeless. The previous year the Board of Trade had withdrawn their approval for it on the grounds of 'a constant failure to communicate'. However, it wasn't until 1898 that the Harrison cord was absolutely outlawed, which would not have been cheering news for two decades of passengers had they known.

Richard had to find some way of coping with the emergency. He had about five seconds to make his decision. The one he made was probably the worst thing he could possibly have done, but was the natural instinct of anyone in his situation. He tried to stop the train.

The problem was that no one at the rear of the train knew

News photographers were still a rarity, but an artist's impression was drawn of the Shipton crash.

anything was wrong. To stop multiple tons of wood and metal hurtling along a line wasn't a case of putting ones foot on the brake. The driver – or in this case the drivers, as there were two engines – had to shut off the steam and throw the engines into reverse. Meanwhile the firemen would apply the tender brakes. But somehow the momentum of the carriages had to be dealt with. The guards at the rear of the train had to brake at their end to slow the carriages in parallel with the engines. Richard blew the alarm whistle to tell the guards to brake, then immediately shut off the steam and reversed. The guards were taken completely by surprise. Before they could even begin braking, Richard had stopped the engines.

The carriages were trapped between their own momentum and two solid, stationery engines. The effect was like a concertina. The ancient carriage with the Oxford passengers was smashed into a pulp instantly. The couplings of the other carriages broke loose. All of which would have been disaster enough, but fate had another twist up her sleeve. Richard had brought the engines to a halt on the Shipton-on-Cherwell canal bridge.

Nine of the fourteen remaining carriages plunged over the edge of the bridge, crashing into the frozen water below or somersaulting onto the banks. When the dust settled, only the two engines and the final two carriages were still on the rails. Thirty-four passengers were dead, and sixty-five badly injured.

That should have been the end of the great Shipton-on-Cherwell railway disaster. Unfortunately, for the injured, it was only the beginning.

They were fortunate that H P Mallam, an Oxford surgeon, was visiting a patient at Shipton Manor, and was soon at the scene improvising splints and applying pressure to wounds to stem the flow of blood. The villagers of Shipton rallied round, as did Lord Randolph Churchill and a house party from Blenheim, while a relief train with helpers and medical supplies was sent out from Oxford. But a base was needed to which the dead and injured could be taken; they couldn't simply be left out in the snow. Luckily the Hampton Gay Paper Mill was nearby. Or perhaps not so luckily....

The mill workers joined in with the other helpers and brought the dead and injured over to the premises. Some of the paper stocks had to be moved out of the way to provide room for the victims to lie down, and blankets and rugs were provided to keep them warm. From somewhere wine and spirits were found to encourage their circulation. The workers rallied round so cheerfully that the Great Western paid them a lump sum in thanks. They were therefore more than a little surprised when the bill arrived.

Pearson, the mill owner, showed himself to be rather distressed that his men had gone off to help the accident victims rather than staying by their machines and getting on with their work. 'Pulp in rag engines destroyed in consequence of the mill hands leaving on the day of the accident to assist the wounded: £15.' He didn't much like having to make room for the bodies either. 'Damage to paper in stock moved to make way for the bodies: £17.' What's more, if the men were engaged in something which didn't make a profit for him – saving people's lives, for example – he didn't see why he should be paying their wages. 'Men's wages, £12 per week for three weeks.' And since he worked there too, he assessed his own wages at £2 per week even though he didn't actually get paid.

Of course it didn't take three weeks to look after the sick and pack them off to hospital, but the dead bodies did hang around between Christmas and New Year.

Particulars of Claim by Mr R. L. Pearson of Hampton Gay Mill, in respect of the Shipton Accident.

To Clothing (blankets & rugs) provided for several of the injured on the line, and, to Wine and Spirits provided for their use on the day of the Accident, and during the time that several of them remained at the Mill House, Telegrams and to Messengers .... 30 ——

30. 0. 0

Pulp in Rag Engines destroyed in consequence of the Mill hands leaving on the day of the Accident to assist the Wounded 15. 0. 0

Pulp in Boilers damaged by fermentation – Damage done to the "Felts" &c in the Paper Machines; and damage to paper in Stock moved to make room for the bodies 17. 0. 0

Injury to Piping, Valves &c by frost   25. 0. 0

Injury to Water Wheel by frost . .   5 —

Loss of business at Messrs Huntley & Palmers Reading, a large quantity of paper being ready to be delivered, but not being delivered at the time was obtained elsewhere 15. 0. 0

The Hampton Gay Paper Mill claim for compensation.

Loss on the Mill, it being idle from Christmas Eve to January the first, during which time the bodies were deposited there; afterwards by frost one week and one week for necessary repairs, say three weeks: £10/10/0d.

Fair enough, there was no reason he should be out of pocket, but one might feel he was trying it on when 'loss on profit of business, calculated at 10 percent on the capital of £2,500 for three weeks' turns up.

What really jolted the Great Western was the realization that the blankets, rugs and alcohol weren't provided out of the kindness of his heart: 'to clothing, blankets and rugs provided to several of the injured on the line, and to wine and spirits provided for their use on the day of the Accident: £30.' Nor was the lump sum given by the Company to his men allowed to interfere: 'whatever was given to the men by the Railway Company was by way of consideration for their services at the accident' – nothing to do with their salaries. The total bill came to £178/14/1d, which really was adding insult to injury.

Still, that was the Great Western's problem. At least the injured had been given shelter, and once they were taken to the Radcliffe Infirmary in Oxford their problems would be over. Or so they might think.

Dr Edward Hussey had been at the Radcliffe Infirmary for twenty years. He was a surgeon of the old school: absolutely opposed to any new developments whatsoever, and not a little corrupt. His greatest achievement was to have himself made simultaneously surgeon and coroner, which meant that he was responsible for investigating his own mistakes on the operating table; unsurprisingly he tended to find that his conduct was invariably above reproach. His particular hatred was reserved for Joseph Lister and his antiseptic system. By use of carbolic acid, Lister had eliminated septic diseases from his wards in Glasgow, and his methods were being taken up by progressive young surgeons all over the country. At the Radcliffe, however, Dr Palmer found it rather difficult to get them past Hussey, who wrote to the hospital board: 'The House seems to be at the mercy of a young house surgeon, who is doing his best to poison the patients with carbolic acid.'

It was into Hussey's hands that the injured from the Shipton disaster fell. He happened to be on duty when they were brought in, and was thereby faced with the difficulty of where to put them. Not a problem; there was one ward with plenty of empty space. For some reason, the other doctors had put a tiny group of patients in there and failed to fill the other beds. What could be more convenient? There was just one snag – the tiny group of patients was suffering from diphtheria.

Hussey didn't believe any of this nonsense about germs. Tiny organisms floating about in the atmosphere, spreading disease from one victim to another – like something by that fellow Jules Verne. He immediately started bundling the half-dead victims in with one of the most virulent conditions of the nineteenth century, where their depressed resistance would have ensured that they were dead before the week was out. Fortunately he was spotted. With considerable difficulty the Matron, Miss Rose Clarributt, and the house surgeon, William Morgan, with the help of George Rolleston (one of the great figures of the Radcliffe, who hated Hussey), managed to dissuade him, and the injured were instead routed to the outpatients' hall, which rapidly became another ward.

Help came flooding in from the most unlikely places – several young men who had met up in the Royal Oak across the road for a convivial Christmas Eve came running across and gave enormous assistance – and in the end only four of the forty-seven died. Dean Liddell, father of Alice Liddell for whom *Alice in Wonderland* was written, sent a letter to *The Times*:

> *While all minds are full of the appalling accident which has marred the happiness of the Season and praise is justly given to the zeal of the surgeons and others who assisted the poor sufferers, I should be glad to claim some acknowledgement for our excellent Matron and the nurses of our Infirmary. I went from the never-to-be-forgotten scene at the station with a message to prepare beds, etc., but all was ready prepared and beef tea, stimulants, hot bottles, hot blankets were all in readiness. Everything was done with a quiet gentleness and order.*

Of course, Liddell was appointed to the hospital board a few weeks later. Politics, politics....

But two good things did come out of the disaster. First, without actually blaming Richard, the enquiry found that his actions had probably caused the disaster. This, they said, was because no one had ever taught the staff how to act in such an emergency. The rule book was rewritten to point out that in a situation of this kind the train must be brought to a halt gradually, without the front brakes being applied – a rule which may well have prevented similar disasters in the future.

Second, the Radcliffe Infirmary was put on a firm financial footing. When the accident took place, it was in serious debt, still looking for subscribers to underwrite its costs. After the disaster, it had them. The Great Western Railway itself contributed £250, and in the Infirmary treasurer's statement for 1875 under 'Donations' appear 'sums paid direct to the Infirmary after the Shipton Accident: £706/15/0d' and 'received through the Committee of the Shipton Accident Fund: £394/18/4d'. So out of the disaster came some good.

And of course a certain factory in Hampton Gay was enabled to continue making its profits. Though whether many of those involved thought that was a good thing is debatable.

The Radcliffe Infirmary, to which the injured from the crash were taken.

CHAPTER 5

The Sunninghill Poachers – Marauders from over the Border 1828

The records of Quarter Sessions in Oxfordshire Record Office contain calendars of prisoners – lists of those who were brought before the justices of the peace and the courts of assize for various crimes within the county and a note of the verdict and punishment handed out. But among them is a record of a case tried entirely at Reading. For the Sunninghill poachers were based in Berkshire, but such a terrible name had they acquired that neighbouring counties were just as scared of them as the Royal County itself, and when they were finally brought to justice gamekeepers along the southern borders of Oxfordshire drew a deep breath of relief that they would not be the next to face some of the most desperate thugs in living memory.

Poaching tends to be thought of today as a lightweight crime; the likeable village rascal slipping out after dark for the odd rabbit or partridge. Careful attention to that old folk song, *The Lincolnshire Poacher*, suggests a different picture:

> *As me and my companions were setting forth a snare*
> *'Twas then we met the gamekeeper, for him we did not care*
> *or we can wrestle and fight, my lads, and jump o'er anywhere...*

Poaching in the eighteenth and nineteenth centuries wasn't a solitary activity; it was carried out by well organized gangs with their own network of receivers and fences. Nor were they too choosy about the methods they used – they could wrestle and fight, and were inclined to use extreme violence to get their own way. The fight between owners and stealers of game was a long one, with vicious tactics used on both sides.

The Game Laws in England were a direct descendant of the forest laws of William the Conqueror, who was harsh in his determination to preserve what he had deemed to be his own game. Disabling a wild beast was punishable by forfeiture of property. In the case of a stag, buck or boar, the perpetrator was to have his eyes put out. By the nineteenth century, even if the Sunninghill Poachers had carried out their business in a polite and amiable manner, they would still have been looking at a death sentence. As it happened, they didn't.

The Poachers were a gang of thirteen – Banditti, they styled themselves – who became so successful that after denuding a game preserve of all they could carry they would write on the wall, 'There are thirteen of us to a man – Catch us who can.' They celebrated the New Year 1828 by attacking the preserves of Prince Leopold at Claremont, beating up the keeper who tried to stop them and stealing not only his money but his clothes. This, as with all their raids, was planned by one Henry Turner of Shrubs Hill, who was the brains behind the whole operation. The gang would meet at his house, fortify themselves with beer and spirits, then set out on the night's work.

The traditional poacher is seen in this Rowlandson cartoon – the poor man trying to feed his wife and children. But the Sunninghill Poachers were more akin to an East End gang of enforcers, letting no one stand in their way

On 6 January 1828 they got through six quarts of beer before setting out to raid Mr Crutchley's estate at Sunninghill – hence the name by which they went down in history – for at least the second and quite possibly the tenth time. Over the previous few weeks there had been numerous attacks on the game there, and three weeks earlier the gamekeeper, Godfrey, had encountered ten of the gang, only to be severely beaten and told, as they left, 'We'll be back!' The whole estate was therefore in a state of readiness, and the raid on 6 January wasn't going to be a walkover.

At half an hour after midnight, Godfrey heard the sound of gunshots as the poachers started to mow down the livestock in the park. He gathered his assistants together and headed towards the noise, which was remarkably brave considering he and his men were armed with sticks and the poachers were quite audibly carrying firearms. Coming out into a clearing, Godfrey found his little band facing a group of men who levelled loaded guns at them and told them to stand off if they knew what was good for them. Godfrey ignored the warning, and his men moved forward. There was a blast from a shotgun and one of them, Mancey, fell to the ground crying out, blood pouring from his thigh. When the click of a second gun being cocked was heard, five of Godfrey's men ran for it, leaving only Godfrey himself, the groaning Mancey, and Glasspool, a bailiff.

The Poachers immediately set on the bailiff, knocking him to the ground and beating him; they thought he was unconscious so they could deal with Godfrey, but he staggered to his feet and managed to walk a few steps. On seeing this, the poachers yelled, 'Shoot the cursed bastard! Curse his eyes, shoot him!' They knocked him to the ground again and clubbed him senseless with their guns, then one of them said, 'Damn him, let's have his boots.' This set a whole chain going, as a second took his neckerchief, a third said 'Let's have his money!', a fourth, 'Let's have his watch!', until they came to his greatcoat, which they couldn't get off. On their way out they yelled triumphantly and took a few more pot-shots at the game. Glasspool's hat was later found torn to shreds some yards away, while Glasspool himself and Mancey had to be taken to the keeper's lodge for medical help.

Crutchley wasn't taking this lying down. He immediately sent down to Bow Street for assistance, and Ruthven, a noted officer on the force, was immediately dispatched. This time there were plenty of witnesses who could swear that Turner had been leading the poachers, and Ruthven swiftly closed in. Turner made a rapid calculation, offered to turn King's Evidence, and promptly betrayed all his gang. Four of them fled just in time; the others found themselves in the cells awaiting trial for malicious wounding, theft and, of course, poaching.

The jury were disinclined to accept Turner's evidence, which was unfortunate as other witnesses were able to identify only Thomas Field, Henry Burnett and Samuel White. The gang, however, had quite another view on Turner in the witness box, interrupting the evidence with 'Damn thee, I wish I had thy neck in a halter and the end over a beam, I'd soon do thy business!' and 'Didn't we all swear to be true blue, and be damned to thee!'. Turner was not a popular man, and the judge insisted on telling him repeatedly how dreadful it was that he was being allowed to escape for turning in the gang, occasionally saying he was going to put him on trial anyway for trying to hedge with his evidence. The trial was a chaotic affair, as none of the accused seemed to be taking it with due solemnity. When one of the witnesses pointed out Field in court and made the mistake of holding his pointing finger a little too near, Field snapped at it, trying to bite it off.

Eventually it was clear that the lack of witness statements meant only Field, Burnett and White could be convicted. The judge certainly wasn't going to let them escape, and quickly passed a death sentence on each of them, rubbing it in with cries of 'Your days are numbered!' and 'The grave will soon open to receive you!', in a way that came disturbingly close to gloating. The five men who escaped conviction showed distressingly little solidarity with their less fortunate colleagues, as their first action on leaving the court was to head for the nearest pub and indulge in drunken merriment. But oddly those who had been condemned didn't seem much more upset.

On their way back to the gaol they were joshing with one another about their execution: 'How shall ye like to be hung,

Tom?', 'Why it's only like wiring a hare – it will be a kick or two and soon over.' They ignored the prison chaplain, and in the days leading up to the hanging complained only of the fact that they only made five shillings each on the haul at Crutchley's estate. The prison authorities thought that being measured up for their coffins would quieten them down a bit, but quite the reverse: 'Hey, Sam, they've had the measuring stick in here.' 'They've been with me too.' 'We'll be had up just at twelve o'clock' – followed by a laugh.

What the authorities were seeing was a phenomenon which would shortly lead to the death penalty being discontinued for most crimes other than murder. The whole point of public executions was to terrify the spectators; to show them some poor wretch terrified at the gallows as a means of preventing them from ever considering a similar crime. Punishment was to be harsh and visible. But it no longer worked that way; a new breed of criminal had arisen, callous and careless of everything including his own life. Now a footpad, a highwayman, a poacher, was quite likely to stand up on the gallows, announce how much he's enjoyed it all, and say he'd do it all again if he got the chance.

Still, Berkshire and the surrounding counties were freed from the threat of the Sunninghill Poachers. With the loss of their presiding genius Henry Turner the gang fell apart and was heard of no more. Neither was Henry Turner, which, given the fact that five people against whom he gave King's Evidence were set free, must give rise to some interesting questions....

CHAPTER 6

Robert Shippen –
A Touch of Light Relief
1710–45

In an era frequently castigated for 'dumbing down', the case of Robert Shippen should ring some warning bells. Electing someone to public office not because you believe they will do the job well, but because their particular bigotry is the same as yours, or worse, because

Robert Shippen – the only surviving likeness.

Brasenose College, from which Shippen conducted his reign of corruption.

you think they'll allow you to get on with your own form of corruption without interference, can backfire rather badly, as the fellows of Brasenose College found when they elected Dr Robert Shippen to be Principal.

On the surface, there was no reason why Shippen should have been considered for the job at all. The election came up in 1710, and Shippen had only taken his degree in 1699 – he was much too young. He was described by Thomas Hearne as sly, lecherous, heavy drinking, self-seeking, corrupt, covetous, unscrupulous, selfish and immoral – and Hearne was one of his friends! True, Shippen was a fellow of the College, but he hadn't exactly distinguished himself in that position. He had been one of the rebels who elected a new Vice Principal of Brasenose against the specific instructions of the college Visitor in 1709, and if that could be seen as standing up for his political principles – he was a confirmed Jacobite – his appointment as Professor of Music at Gresham College could not. He knew nothing whatsoever about music, and when he finally resigned he did so in favour of his brother who was a medical doctor – not exactly an expert in harmony.

So what recommended Shippen to the fellows? They had a perfectly good candidate in the shape of Dr Smith, Principal of Hart Hall, but unfortunately he was described as 'a man of learning and a good disciplinarian' – not at all what they seem to have been looking for. Shippen, by contrast, had been wheedling his way into the fellows' affections by telling them that he wouldn't be expecting anything in the way of hard work from them, or any great scholarship. In fact, said Hearne, 'they expect to live easy under him', and when the election was held on 2 June 1710 Shippen won by one vote.

It was at this point that the fellows began to realize that a man who was prepared to let them indulge their vices probably had a few vices of his own to indulge. It's one thing to have a blind eye turned to your corruption; quite another to discover that you've put yourself in the hands of someone who is himself corrupt. Even the slower among them must have got an inkling of what was going on when Shippen's brother distinguished himself by being one of the few men in the eighteenth century to be sent to the Tower for treason; but by then the most ruthless Principal the college has ever suffered was well into his stride.

His first step was to move in on the college livings. Like most Oxford and Cambridge colleges, Brasenose had acquired the right of presentation to various livings around the country – that is, when a clergyman connected with a given church died, they had the right to appoint his successor. There was a logic in this. With the single exception of the Principal, no fellow of a college was allowed to be married; since many of them did eventually marry, they needed a new career outside the academic world. And this was what the college kept the livings for: as jobs for the fellows when they left the college. What they most definitely did not keep the livings for was as additional income for the Principal while he was in office. Shippen thought otherwise.

The first living whose income he took over was St Mary's Whitechapel. Traditionally one was supposed to wait for the existing clergyman to leave, but Shippen couldn't be bothered with petty details like that. He committed what the Whitechapel parishioners described as 'a theft and a violence' by simply throwing the current holder of the living out. Then he took over the living of Stepney, and followed that with Great Billing. It was a useful way of increasing his income – all the livings had a salary attached – but too slow. He needed something which would bring him in a fortune at a sweep. And the solution was obvious: now that he was Principal he had the right to marry, and he intended to marry money.

The money in question was Frances, the widow of Sir Gilbert Clarke. She was a good match for Shippen; he was her fourth husband and she had built her fortune up through the first three. Now she clearly felt she was rich enough and had the title she wanted – she continued to be known as Lady Clarke for the rest of her life – so she could indulge herself with a toy-boy. Shippen was seventeen years her junior. The fellows soon discovered that if Shippen was unpleasant his wife could be insufferable. 'She was a very proud woman, given much to drinking and gaming, and did no good,' notes Hearne. To other people perhaps not, but she certainly did some good for herself.

She turned out to be just as corrupt as Shippen himself. Although not needing any salaried positions herself, she started doling out those to which Shippen had access to her own toadies and creatures. Simpson, the Head Cook of the college, got his post at her instigation, and when he died the job was given to his son. This wouldn't have mattered if the son had been a decent chef, but he wasn't, for which he could hardly be blamed as he was only two years old. The child died a year later, possibly because some of the fellows were desperate for a decent meal.

Naturally such an august woman could not be expected to live in the existing Principal's Lodgings. Shippen annexed all the rooms in the south-east corner of the Old Quad to add to his existing accommodation, and ended up with pretty well the entire eastern block of the college – the gatehouse wall – as his own living quarters. Not that he spent a great deal of time in them. He had to go and visit Whitechapel, Stepney and Great Billing some time, on top of which he had houses in Appleton and London, so that as the college historian R W Jeffrey observes, 'the College must really have been a mere place of call'.

Lady Clarke brought Shippen £500 a year, for which he must have been very grateful; there was a good deal of malicious chuckling in 1728 when she died on the way back from a journey to Bath and the money ceased. On the other hand, she was the best part of two decades older than him, so the comfort he gained in board he lost in bed. Or did he? Shippen was notorious as a lecher, and would probably have had difficulty fitting his wife in.

One of his most famous conquests was Mrs Churchill, the wife of an Oxford bookbinder, and reputed to be one of the prettiest women in England, at least at the beginning of the relationship. Unfortunately many of Shippen's sexual activities were conducted in such places as St Thomas's parish, the notorious red light district of Oxford, and he was riddled with the pox. This he duly transferred to his victim, who died of it in a miserable condition. No one was ever able to turn it into a formal charge against Shippen, but it was frequent gossip in the town for years afterwards.

Not as much, however, as Shippen's masterpiece of corruption and lechery: the case of the Ashmolean election. In 1731 he was one of the six Proctors who were to elect a new Keeper of the Ashmolean in a strongly contested fight. The two front-runners were John Andrews of Magdalen College and George Huddesford, President of Trinity College. Shippen supported Huddesford, for reasons which may not have been entirely connected with his suitability for the job, but on this occasion he lost – Andrews was inducted into the post on 14 April 1731. And that should have been the end of it, except that Shippen didn't take kindly to being beaten, particularly given what was at stake for himself.

Shortly afterwards there was a change of Proctors, which would have given Huddesford a significant majority over Andrews – but of course it was too late. Or was it? Shippen got to work. Ensuring that the majority of the Proctors were now firmly behind Huddesford, he got to work undermining Andrews. Eventually he terrified the poor man so much that on 14 February 1732 – Valentine's Day as it happens – a strange ceremony took place. Shippen and Huddesford visited Andrews in the Ashmolean, and in exchange for £50 Andrews

Trinity College, home of George Huddesford, who was willing to pay highly to take over the Ashmolean.

handed over the keys to Huddesford and slunk out of the building. The President of Trinity had taken over the Ashmolean without any legitimate election taking place.

Shippen wasn't going to all this trouble out of concern for the great museum, still less out of friendship for Huddesford. He had a much more self-interested motive. Shortly afterwards it became noticeable that he was paying visits to Huddesford's unusually attractive wife, generally when her husband was out. In fact, the fellows of Trinity realized that their President was actually getting out of the way whenever Shippen turned up, and understood just what Huddesford had offered Shippen to get him the Keepership. How Mrs Huddesford felt about being payment for her husband's appointment is not recorded.

The fellows of Brasenose had elected Shippen, and they were stuck with him for thirty-five years, until his death in 1745 – at which point, incidentally, he was still holding the livings of Whitechapel and Great Billing. Corruption was not entirely uncommon in the eighteenth century. Robert Walpole, the Prime Minister, seems to have been of the opinion that a major reason for holding public office was to cream off as much capital as possible. But in case anyone should believe that the academic world was above that sort of thing, take note of the saga of Robert Shippen – and of the way that having opened the door to corruption, it can be very difficult to shut it out again.

CHAPTER 7

Mary Blandy – Hanging Them Not Too High
1751

One gets into the habit of thinking of murderers as the dregs of society: seedy poachers, sinister highwaymen, members of gangs of thugs who would as soon slit your throat as steal your watch. Perhaps that was why it came as such a shock to Oxfordshire when they discovered they had in their midst a murderer who was not only from a superior social class, but was quite an attractive young lady to boot.

Mary Blandy was described by those who had no reason to wish her well as

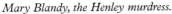

Mary Blandy, the Henley murdress.

of a middle size, well shaped, of a brown complexion, with black eyes full of fire; and though not a beauty ... very agreeable, especially when she speaks, and her conversation is full of wit and good sense.

She was also getting on in years, at least by the standards of the mid-eighteenth century, having just turned thirty and hence moving rapidly beyond marriageable age. In her case the biological clock turned into a biological time bomb, with fatal results for the man who tried to stand in her way.

Francis Blandy, her father, was the Town Clerk of Henley-on-Thames, and a highly respected man in the community. He was part of Henley's social elite, on good terms with gentlemen and their families, and when his wife died in 1749 he did not cease entertaining except for the formal period of mourning. He still had his only child, Mary, as hostess, and no one could deny that she saw the cream of local society passing through her sitting room.

There was some calculation in this. Francis, like most men of his era, was concerned to make his daughter a good match, and for all her charms she seemed unable to ensnare the right man. The older she grew, the more desperate the situation became, until Blandy decided to weight the scales. He was known to be a man of honour and good position; why should

The main street in Henley, showing the house where Francis Blandy lived with his daughter.

Mary Blandy's last flight: the bridge in Henley.

he not also be one of fortune? He decided to exaggerate his daughter's expectations a little, claiming that he was worth £12,000, all of which would eventually descend to his only child and her fortunate husband. Then he settled back to see which of his extended social circle would take the bait.

Typically, it was the last one he wanted. Captain Cranston, a Scottish army officer, was not even particularly good looking, and if he had social graces they were those of a lounge-lizard. But this wasn't the reason why Blandy warned his daughter off the man. Rumours had reached him that Cranston was married, and had a wife still living in Scotland; indeed, that he had come south specifically to take advantage of a loophole which enabled him to claim his marriage wasn't valid, contract another with a rich heiress, and take the resultant fortune back to his first wife. Better that Mary should live out her life unmarried than become entangled with such a man. Unfortunately Blandy was hoist with his own petard. His lies about his fortune had drawn Cranston's attention, and he could hardly deny them now without becoming a laughing stock and destroying his daughter's chances for ever.

Mary, on the other hand, had at last found a man who wanted her, and was not about to let him go. Her father's warnings were simply shrugged off. Blandy had no choice: he had allowed Cranston entry to his house but now he had to bar him. Cranston returned to Scotland, still determined to get his hands on Blandy's £12,000. Mary was distraught, deprived of her lover. The scene was set for murder as neatly as in any Golden Age detective novel.

It was on a morning at the beginning of August 1751 that a package arrived at the Blandy household from Scotland. Addressed to Mary, it contained some Scots pebbles to be made into earrings, together with a packet of white powder to clean them. The term 'Scots pebbles' was to send a chill down the spine of any respectable inhabitant of Henley for years to come, but in fact the significant aspect of the package was the white powder. Subsequent events suggested that it was probably arsenic, and that the pebbles had merely been a device for introducing it into the house.

Mary was in the habit of mixing up water gruel for her father, and on 5 August she made him his usual bowl. On this occasion, however, she seems to have slipped some of the white powder into it. No one noticed this at the time, and if Francis Blandy was anything to go by it would be difficult to prove; the man must have had the constitution of an ox. However, he failed to finish the bowl and left it lying on the table. Few external servants in the eighteenth century would have survived without the understood system of perks. Candle ends, cast off clothing, and unfinished food were how they made ends meet. On this occasion it was Mrs Hemmet, the washerwoman who tended to the family, who spotted the half-full bowl and helped herself.

It was very nearly the last thing she ever did. Shortly afterwards she was carried home in a chair, groaning and vomiting. 'She continued dangerously ill for a long time, that her life was despaired of', said a contemporary writer, 'but she is now able to walk abroad, though it is thought she will never recover so as to be quite well again.' Mrs Hemmet's diet was not so wide-ranging that it was difficult to guess what had disagreed with her, and the first inklings of suspicion that something was not quite right began to appear.

Either Mary had to give up immediately or press on as fast as possible. She chose the latter. The following day's water gruel was sent up to Blandy's room, and once again he failed to finish it; the remains were sent back down to the kitchen. Mary happened to be there and stuck a spoon in the mixture, apparently searching for something. She pulled the spoon out covered in white sediment, which had sunk to the bottom; the mystery of Francis Blandy's unusually high resistance to poison was solved. Suddenly she realised that the kitchen staff were all looking at her. 'The oatmeal looks very white today', she observed carelessly, and hurriedly left the kitchen. But the staff remembered Mrs Hemmet, and were beginning to think the unthinkable.

Meanwhile Mary was in trouble. If the powder was going to sink to the bottom of the gruel every time, and if Blandy insisted on eating only half way down the bowl, there was no way she could poison him. There had to be a different method of administering it. Clearly it couldn't be in anything she too would have to eat. The idea of dissolving it in Blandy's cup of tea came to her, but the practice proved more difficult. The powder would thin out but not dissolve, as had been proved by the gruel, and the result was a cup of tea filled with what appeared to be grit. She poured the poisoned tea out of the window and set to thinking of another way.

Unfortunately she was a lady of leisure, and had never thought to wash up dirty crockery; that was what the staff were for. She simply left the tainted cup on the table. Not all the staff were too keen on washing up either, and when Susannah Gunnell, the chambermaid, decided to treat herself to a cup of tea she used the dirty cup she found without washing it out first. The punishment was out of all proportion to the crime. 'Though she is now quite recovered,' said the commentator, 'she is wore down to a skeleton.' More significantly, from Mary's point of view, it was becoming increasingly obvious that eating and drinking in the Blandy household were fraught with danger.

Even Francis Blandy's luck was beginning to run out. His health was clearly deteriorating, and he complained of bowel pains – what was more, his teeth were falling out, a common side-effect of arsenic poisoning. Had it been just the master of the house, the servants might have been sympathetic but unsuspicious; taken in conjunction with Mrs Hemmet and

Susannah Gunnell the whole thing looked very sinister. They consulted together and decided to do what was almost unthinkable – to go to a friend of the family and tell her their suspicions that their mistress was poisoning her father. The friend in question was a Mrs Mountney, who sent for Mr Norton, the local apothecary, and asked him to test the white powder which the staff were collecting from various pots and dishes in which Blandy's food had been served. This was outside Norton's usual sphere, and he failed to identify it. 'But let it be what it will,' he said, 'sure that stuff has no business there.'

Mary was doing herself no favours. Referring to her father as 'a toothless old rogue' was tactless enough, but telling the cook that she was sure he would be dead before October was criminally stupid. When asked how she was so sure, she stammered out that Cranston had visited a conjuror in Scotland who had told him one of the family would die about that time. It convinced no one.

The irony was that Blandy knew what was happening. When the servants tried to tell him what Mary was up to, they realized he already knew. 'Poor, lovesick girl', he said. 'What will not a woman do for the man she loves?' The poison was too well entrenched within his system for him to be saved now. On 9 August he came down from his room to the kitchen and faced his daughter. 'About this time of the year Queen Anne was poisoned', he said. 'I remember that a long while ago, being in company at the Red Lion, they gave us some damned stuff to drink which poisoned us all. One died, and I was very sick with it.' He fixed his daughter with a look. 'I am afraid it will be my lot to be poisoned.'

Mary forced a smile. 'Papa, it is twenty years ago since that happened. I remember it very well.' She turned and hurriedly left the room. Blandy picked up the cup of tea she had made for him, and poured it into the cat's bowl.

It was too late to save him. From that point he kept to his room and only saw his daughter one more time. 'My dear girl,' he said to her as she sat on the foot of his bed, 'I forgive you with all my heart, but will hang Cranston if I can. Be gone!' He died on 14 August.

Blandy's death brought matters to a head, but not in the way that might be expected. The servants were sure his daughter was poisoning him; they had set rumours flying about the town, and Mr Littleton, Blandy's clerk, had actually accused her of it to her face. After his final meeting with her, Blandy had confined her to her room with two men watching her. But now he was dead, she was free. Absolute mistress of the house, she could do whatever she wished, including dismissing the servants who had spread tales about her. The two men watching her were sent away, and there was nothing they could do about it. Tradition dictated that one of the servants should sit up with her the night after her father's death, but she refused to allow it. Mary Blandy was in control now, and she knew exactly what she was going to do.

The plan had all gone wrong. Her father was supposed to die quietly of some unspecified illness; she would be the grieving daughter, then after a decent interval marry Cranston. Now everyone in Henley was whispering about how she had murdered him, and at some point the authorities were bound to take notice. What she needed was privacy in which to destroy all the evidence before facing down her accusers.

She collected together all Cranston's letters, including the one received on the day of her father's death, which had been opened by the doctors and which read, 'Above all, don't spare the powder, in order to keep the pebbles clean', and burned them in the kitchen grate. In addition, the servants noticed, she threw on a small packet of powder which burned with a bluish flame; on raking it out after she had gone, they found it was marked 'Powder for cleaning the Scotch pebbles'. Or so they said; if it had actually contained arsenic, burning it would have produced gases not calculated to do any good to the inhabitants of the kitchen. It is rather of a piece with her reported remark: 'Now I am pretty easy', which belongs in one of the popular theatrical melodramas of the time. Could the servants be seeing what they wanted to see, in the conviction of her guilt?

What was certainly true was that she offered £500 to her servant, Richard Harman, to get her away, but even that wasn't necessarily suspicious. Lynch mobs weren't that uncommon – three years later a visitor to Oxford was to be beaten half to death for accidentally having the wrong colour bridle on his horse during a rather violently contested election – and Blandy had been a popular man. The question of her guilt wouldn't come into it. And as for her accusers, they were on decidedly shaky ground.

Harman had told Littleton about the attempted bribe, but Littleton knew enough law to realize that nothing could be done about it. As long as Mary had not been formally accused of murder, any action taken against her would itself be criminal. Yet he didn't want Blandy's murderer to get away. He got some of his friends together and stationed them at her front door to stop her if she did try to escape, but a local lawyer to whom he went for advice told him it was actually illegal for them to be in her house unless she had given explicit permission. He then went to see the Mayor of Henley, who was meeting with the Corporation at the Catherine Wheel, and asked him to send a constable to watch her. This the Mayor did, but on arriving the constable refused to have anything to do with the affair, on the grounds that Mary hadn't been committed to his custody. Everyone knew the story, and yet it seemed she was going to get away with it.

Oddly enough, it was fear of the illegal mob which trapped her. Scared to leave the house without protection, she tried to get various servants to help her but they all refused. Had she left the house that night, who knows what might have happened? But she daren't, and when she slipped out the next morning with £1,000 in her bag the mob saw her go. By the time she had reached Henley churchyard they were following. She ran for the bridge over the river, followed by an interested crowd who thought she might be about to throw herself in, and on reaching the other side took refuge in the Angel alehouse, where she was discovered by the officers of Henley Corporation calmly consuming a pint of wine and a toast.

The mob had given the Corporation the excuse they needed. Claiming that they were simply protecting her, and in no way accusing her of anything, they brought her back across the river and to her own house. Meanwhile Francis Blandy's body was being rushed to the coroner, where it was discovered that he had indeed been poisoned. There was a case to answer, and Mary Blandy was charged with murder.

Her immediate line of defence was that she had indeed fed the powder to her father – there were too many witnesses to deny that – but had not realized what it was. Cranston had told her it was a love philtre to make Blandy more affectionate towards her so that he would withdraw his objections to her marriage. It sounded lame for an educated woman, and she was committed to Oxford Gaol for trial.

However, Mary was no ordinary prisoner. This was the daughter of the Town Clerk of Henley, even if she had murdered him. The magistrates of Oxford were regular visitors at her house, and she had often taken tea with them. Whatever the facts of the case, the social proprieties must be seen to be observed. She was allowed to delay her arrival in gaol to enable her to pack all the clothes which she would need for her stay there. A serving woman, Mrs Dean, was allowed to go with her to the gaol to ensure she was well looked after, and she took her own tea chest with her, as it was full of the finest hyson. When she arrived, she asked if she was to be fettered, and on being told not if she behaved well, she replied, 'I have wore them all this morning in the coach.'

Mary Blandy takes civilized tea with a friend – but note the fetters peeping out under her skirt.

Indeed, her time in the gaol was not unlike a civilized stay in a country house. She would walk in the Governor's garden, refuse to be seen by any but her particular friends, and play at cards in the evening. But the polite social mask covered one stark fact: the evidence against her was damning, and there was no chance of an acquittal. Just once she commented on Cranston, who had fled the country on hearing of her arrest and the warrant out for his own. 'I pray to God they may take the villain, that he may suffer,' she said, 'for it is all owing to his request and advice.' It was while in the gaol that she learned of the final irony – that the £12,000 for which Cranston had urged her to murder her father didn't exist. Francis Blandy was worth at the most £4,000. His attempt to claim otherwise had led directly to his death.

Finally she faced the court in the Divinity School, now part of the Bodleian, and the inevitable verdict of guilty. Before her execution she made one final request: that she should not be hanged too high for the sake of decency. Female executions always drew a crowd of dubious types, eager for a look up a woman's skirts as she dangled from the gallows. With that she went to her death. The evening of her execution, her body was brought back to Henley in a hearse, and quietly buried at eleven at night in the chancel of Henley church beside the father she had killed. His burial and hers are recorded on the same page of the Henley parish register.

The burials of Mary and the father she murdered sit opposite one another in the Henley parish register.

For once there is some poetic justice in the story. Cranston had fled the country for France, but he didn't last long. On arriving in Boulogne he applied for protection from a Mrs Ross, an old friend of his family. Unfortunately he had old enemies too. His treatment of his real wife in Scotland had outraged her family, and they let it be known that once they got their hands on him his life would be worth less than that of Francis Blandy. Fearing that they were closing in on him, he went on the run once again, ending up in Flanders, where he was known by no one.

This had its disadvantages; he had no access to money or friends, and would have starved if his brother had not kept him on the poverty line. His own money had been seized on by the Lords of Session in Scotland, and most of it diverted to the support of his wife. Desperate for a way out, he applied to the Father of a local convent, portrayed himself as a penitent sinner, and asked for shelter with them. This he was granted, but not for long; scarcely had he arrived when he fell ill with an odd sickness – all his limbs swelled up, 'that it was thought by those about him he must have burst. And thus, after about nine days illness, he expired in the most agonizing torments and, as some say, raving mad.'

So the Mary Blandy story ended like a Jacobean tragedy, with all the principal participants dead, and in a very satisfactory manner suffering punishment for their misdeeds. Still, one wonders about Mary's story that she believed the powder to be a love potion to make her father fonder of her. Perhaps it was at that – there can be few fathers who, aware that their daughter is poisoning them, continue to let her prepare their meals and forgive her everything. Or was it just that, knowing what he now did about Mary, Blandy no longer thought he had any reason to go on living?

The devious Captain Cranston, Mary's lover.

CHAPTER 8

The Crime of Noah Austin – A Study in Responsibility 1863

T he value of archives as evidence largely depends on their survival. That's a pretty obvious thing to say, but it's amazing how often people forget it. If nothing survives there's no evidence and no story, something rather difficult to get round; but if something survives it's rather too easy to lose sight of the possibility that there might be other evidence which didn't make it. And that the other evidence might change the emphasis of the story. Fortunately, sometimes the missing evidence turns up later.

Noah Austin was the son of a respectable farmer in a small way, living in Upper Heyford; he himself followed the trade of butcher in a rather erratic manner. He was rather taken with Elizabeth Allen, a young woman of twenty-five, the daughter of James Allen, the local miller. However, Allen wasn't entirely comfortable with Austin paying court to his daughter; although he didn't go so far as to forbid Austin his house, he did everything he could to discourage him, and even refused to give him the tenancy of a beer house which was in his

Bicester market place, where Noah made his fatal arrangement with James Allen.

control. Nevertheless Austin visited Elizabeth several times a week, and the father made no active move against him.

On 13 February 1863 both Allen and Austin's father made their usual trips to Bicester market, Allen taking with him a neighbour called Grantham, and Austin senior taking Noah. During the afternoon, the son left a message for his father with the ostler of the Cross Keys Inn not to wait for him as he was planning to walk home; he'd felt rather cold on the drive in that morning. However, far from walking he went straight round to the White Hart where he found Allen in the act of receiving a cheque for £12. He asked Allen for a sample of oats, claiming his father wanted to buy some, but then returned a few minutes later saying his father had already left and could he possibly beg a lift home?

Allen wasn't too happy as he felt he owed Grantham a lift back, but in fact Grantham had made his own arrangements, and so Allen and Noah left Bicester at about five-thirty. They stopped at the Jersey Arms, Middleton, for a glass of brandy, and then kept on the turnpike road to pay a brief visit to a farmer named Meacock in Caulcott who was to thrash some barley for the miller. Two of Meacock's labourers saw Austin standing by the cart while the transaction was taking place, and Meacock was the last witness to see Allen alive.

As Allen and Austin drove off, the two labourers set out for home; they had not gone more than half a mile when they heard two shots from the direction of the road. The shots were also heard by two lads called Buckland, who were driving some pigs along the track which ran parallel to the turnpike

Now better known as a former air base, Upper Heyford was a little village when Noah Austin lived there.

road; they decided not to investigate but 800 yards further on were startled when Austin rushed past them and off in the direction of Upper Heyford. Noah ran straight to his own house, but then changed his mind and went to find Wooloff, the carter at Allen's mill, and told him to go and meet his master on the Caulcott road. Wooloff duly set out, and found Allen's horse and cart fastened to a gate; to his horror, a few yards further on, he found Allen himself with two bullets in his brain – evidently, from the singed hair, fired at very close quarters. His pockets had been turned out and only sixpence remained. Meanwhile Austin had gone to visit Elizabeth, and after a brief trip home for tea returned to visit her again.

When news of Allen's death reached the village, Noah was the obvious suspect. He said he'd left Allen in perfect health; two men had stopped them on the road to pay for meal and he'd decided to get down and walk. He added, muddying the water, that two other men had passed them a couple of minutes earlier. Lots of possible suspects. Unfortunately, when Noah was searched, a number of gun caps were found in his pocket. He was asked to accompany the officers of the law to Oxford.

It was at this point that Austin made a serious tactical error – he asked for permission to call on Elizabeth Allen to pick up the key to his box, which he had lent to her. The authorities had no intention of allowing any such thing, but they were interested to find out why their suspect was so keen to get the key into his possession. They picked up the key from Elizabeth themselves and opened the box. Inside it were £15 in money, and a purse and key which Allen was known to have taken with him to Bicester. The authorities promptly mounted a more extensive search, and found a revolver with three of its shots discharged, concealed in Austin senior's gig.

The trial was brief and to the point; the judge stated that he was as certain Austin had killed James Allen as if he had seen him do it with his own eyes, a remark which left the jury in no doubt as to where their duty lay. Noah Austin was duly condemned, still claiming he was innocent, and the only question which remained in the minds of those involved was how he expected to gain the hand of a woman whose father he had obviously murdered.

Austin received visits in the condemned cell from his sisters and Elizabeth, but it seemed unlikely he would see his own father. The old man was already infirm, and seemed crushed by the turn of events. This was a matter of considerable annoyance to the authorities, who rather counted on his father extracting a confession; they were never entirely comfortable with people going to the gallows still protesting their innocence. Then, to everyone's surprise, on 18 March Austin suddenly changed his mind and made a voluntary statement to the Reverend Philip Wynter, one of the local justices, in his cell. What surprised people even more was the light it threw on his motives:

I did not buy the pistol with the intention of shooting Mr Allen. On Wednesday the 11th of February Mr Allen had behaved ill to his daughter by turning her out of doors. She sent for me on the following morning and after telling me of his treatment said she wished some accident would happen to him. I said, 'I shall see, but we shall be found out.' She said, 'Oh, no, we shall not; be sure you come down in the evening and we will arrange it.' My impression was she wished her father to be got rid of.

I went to the mill again on Thursday evening and saw Miss Allen; she again said she wished that something would happen to her father. More words passed between us, but I do not remember exactly what they were. Her father then came in tipsy, and I felt anxious to avoid a quarrel, as when he was in that state he could not say anything against me bad enough. I felt sure that Miss Allen wished me to get rid of her father, and I left the mill with the intention of carrying out what I believed to be her wish; but I do not think she knew that I should do so the next day, though I am sure she thought I should do so at some time.

I then determined to go to Bicester the next day with my father for the purpose. I carried the pistol in my pocket. I could not have done it unless I had had some drink. I went to a strange house in Bicester that I might not be known, either the Nag's Head or the King's Head, and had about two glasses of strong beer. I then returned with Mr Allen, as stated in the evidence, and while sitting by his side raised the pistol to his cheek and fired the first shot, which caused him at once to fall over the off side of the cart. While he was falling I fired the other shot, and when he was lying on the ground I took the purse out of his pocket. There were only a few shillings in it. I knew he had the £5 note and the cheque in his breast pocket but I did not want his money. I took the purse to make it appear that he had been robbed as well as murdered.

I tied the horse to the gate, as stated in the evidence, and on the way to the mill I placed the pistol in my father's gig, and then went to the mill, and afterwards returned home and then went up to my sister's bedroom and put the purse and the key in my desk, as found by the police. I make this statement because I wish to ease the mind of my poor, afflicted father.

None of which exonerated Austin, but it suddenly made life extremely sticky for Elizabeth Allen. She rapidly visited the Clerk of the Peace, John Marriott Davenport, to produce some letters Noah had written her, which she hoped would clear her from any charge of complicity; while she was in his office a crowd gathered in the street outside, bent on giving her an extremely unpleasant reception when she emerged, but she spotted them and left by a different route. Whatever the letters said, the evidence against her was not strong enough to proceed. Yet Austin's story did explain the problem which had been puzzling people; why he should suddenly decide after all that time to kill Allen, when there was nothing in it for him.

Another story subsequently emerged from Wooloff which fitted in with the rest of the evidence. On the night prior to his murder, Allen was in a public house in a nearby village, and when he failed to arrive home his carter came looking for him. Allen admitted that he was nervous of walking home alone, not because of Austin, whose plans were unknown, but because there had been a spate of garrottings in the neighbourhood. Wooloff walked back with him, and along the way they saw Austin lurking behind a hedge. The carter's presence seems to have bought Allen another few hours of life.

If Austin had not felt the need to put his father's mind at rest, the story of Elizabeth Allen's involvement would never have come out, and Noah would have gone down as a muddled criminal who couldn't even see his own best interests. Which leads one to wonder how many times such things have happened because the vital piece of evidence which provides the real motivation has been missing.

CHAPTER 9

PC28 Joseph Gilkes – A Policeman's Lot Is Not a Happy One 1869

The English have always been ambivalent on the subject of the police. Infringement of the personal liberties of the subject, they tend to cry, just before calling the boys in blue round to investigate a burglary. Basically what we want is a police force that leaves us alone to do exactly what we want, while preventing everyone else from doing things we don't like, which doesn't really work.

When Robert Peel remodelled the London police in 1829 it was to a chorus of objections, but gradually the reforms spread around the country, reaching Oxford forty years later. Up to that point, policing in Oxford had been run on the most eccentric lines. The City of Oxford, as embodied in the Mayor and Aldermen, had the power of watch and ward within the boundaries during the day. However, all their men went off duty at 9.00pm sharp, which would have been a thieves' charter had the job not been taken over at that point by the University police, known as the Oxford City Night Police. To say that two completely separate police forces was inconvenient is an understatement; finally one united force was created by the Oxford Police Act of 1868, and appeared on the streets on 1 January 1869.

Police wearing the uniform which might have saved Gilkes.

At the best of times it was a tough life. Drunkenness and being found asleep on duty were punishable by instant dismissal. Neither was entirely outside the realm of possibility, as the hours were long, there were no days off, and policemen were forbidden to return to the station during their tour of duty unless they were bringing in a prisoner or a report. This meant they had to grab food and drink as they did their rounds, which in turn usually meant a deal with the pubs on their beat. They were badly paid, even by the standards of the time – 17 shillings rising to £1 a week for a constable – and any man who was certified sick had a shilling a day deducted from his pay.

The uniform for the first year was a greatcoat, a dress tunic, a cape, two pairs of trousers, two pairs of boots, a police helmet, a stock and an armlet, but that presupposed there was a uniform available. New recruits sometimes had to wait, and it may well have been this which had fatal consequences for Joseph Gilkes.

Gilkes had been born at Great Rollright and was on the Metropolitan Police before coming to join the new force in Oxford. He was twenty-two, and had joined up on 5 January 1869. Less than a month later he was dead.

At about 7.45 on the evening of 4 February, PC28 Gilkes and his colleague PC30 Thomas Wilkes were proceeding down St Ebbes Street and along Commercial Road when they noticed a crowd of people, mainly women and children, standing across the footway in front of Mr Axtell's shop in Blackfriars Road, waiting to be served with meat. As they were

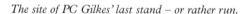

The site of PC Gilkes' last stand – or rather run.

blocking the thoroughfare, Gilkes went up to them and told them to move along. It may be that his lack of uniform prevented the crowd realizing that he was a policeman, or it may be they just didn't like being ordered about. At any rate, a Mrs Cox replied, 'Who are you? We shall do as we like', and proceeded to abuse him. Gilkes took hold of her by the shoulder, propelling her towards the road, when she fell down in a sitting position and Gilkes' authority was severely eroded.

Her husband John Sims Cox, a tailor of Gas Street, promptly struck Gilkes in the face, knocking him down into the road from which Mrs Cox had just jumped up, and the pair of them started to beat him and pull him about. Gilkes staggered against the wall, whereupon Mrs Cox struck him on the back of the head with a dish she was carrying, yelling, 'Take that, you bugger!' The dish broke against the wall and Gilkes received a severe gash on the head. At this point he began to realize the crowd was not on his side.

He started to walk – or stagger – away down Blackfriars Road, then moved up into a run as the crowd flooded after him. James Blay, Keziah Cox's brother, was in the crowd and was seen by witnesses standing in the middle of the road shouting, 'Give it to him!' Sarah Hunt of Commercial Row saw the mob chasing Gilkes, and a little later her son arrived home carrying the man's hat, which had been left behind in the fight. Subsequently Keziah Cox turned up and demanded it, apparently as a trophy, boasting of how she'd served Gilkes and how she'd have given him ten times more if anyone had helped her.

Meanwhile, Henry Lunnon, who was drinking in the tap room of Beckley's Beer Shop further down the road, heard a commotion and cries of 'Stop the thief!', which suggests the crowd were a little confused about what was happening; he rushed out into the street and saw Gilkes running, so he started in pursuit. He yelled after the fleeing policeman, 'Stop, my man, no one shall hurt you', to which Gilkes yelled back, 'I can't – they'll kill me!' He dashed past Trinity Church, but already must have realized he was in an impossible position – there was no exit off Blackfriars Road which wasn't a dead end, and the road itself led down to the river.

Lunnon himself misjudged where the water started and ran in up to his knees in the darkness. According to another pursuer, William Wakelin, Gilkes had already gone in up to his waist; Wakelin called to him to come back, but getting no reply ran off with another man named Cripps to get a punt and rescue the constable. By the time they got the punt to the spot there was no sign of Gilkes. His body was found floating in the water two hours later, about thirty yards away from where he'd gone in.

What was Wilkes doing while all this happened? The coroner was very interested in this question, and it transpired that the answer was: trying to blend into the background. He did nothing to help Gilkes, then followed the crowd as far as Trinity Church, but losing sight of his colleague turned and went home. The coroner was not amused. If Wilkes had helped, he said, the tragedy might have been averted; Wilkes clearly thought it might have been doubled. The Superintendent was obviously of the opinion that Wilkes was not the stuff of which good policemen are made, and dismissed him a few days later.

As for Gilkes, the Coroner's verdict was 'drowned whilst escaping from Keziah Cox, her husband John Sims Cox, and James Blay, when being violently assaulted by them'. The evidence didn't warrant a charge of murder, and it was clear that

The police occurrence book, which laconically notes, among lost dogs and found bags, the death of a constable by drowning.

the Oxford Police had a long way to go in earning the respect of the populace. Only four days later, PC20 William Boulter found four young men in Cornmarket at two in the morning, ringing doorbells and causing a disturbance; when he told them to go home quietly, 'they replied they should ring the bells if they thought proper'. Less than a week after that, Inspector Barratt was attacked and knocked down in the same street by three youths, at least one of whom proved to be a student at Queens.

It's easy to think of the early twenty-first century as being a period of increased lawlessness, but the events of barely more than a century ago put it into context. St Ebbes was a poor area, a warren of alleyways and slum housing, where even policemen going around in pairs were not safe. Something called Blackfriars Road still exists, roughly on the line of a section of its predecessor, but the housing is modern, part of the St Ebbes clearance scheme of thirty years ago. Commercial Row and Gas Street have vanished for ever. Difficult to think of the area just down from the Ice Rink as the place where a policeman lost his life at the hands of a mob – but worth remembering when we get too cynical about our own age.

Old St Ebbes, showing Blackfriars Road, in the nineteenth century.

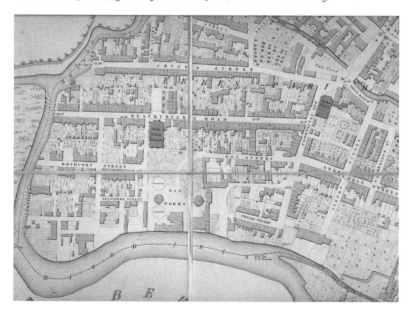

CHAPTER 10

Lowe v Lowe – An All-too-everyday Story of Country Folk 1592

Getting out of a loveless marriage was not easy before the nineteenth century. Although a law of 1539 intended to make divorce simpler to obtain, this was a relative term; divorce required an Act of Parliament, and few but the nobility could afford to proceed along those lines. Between the Reformation and 1857, when the commissioners on the law of divorce issued their first report, there had been precisely 317 divorces in England; during the next ten years 1,279 marriages were dissolved. What this meant in practical terms was that prior to the mid-nineteenth century a lot of couples, particularly the poorer ones, were forced to stay together when it might have been better for all parties if they hadn't.

However, one other form of pseudo-divorce was possible: a judicial separation *a mensa et thoro*, which basically meant that the couple were separated in bed and board. Some fairly grim activities were required for this to be feasible, like those evident in the case of Michael and Joane Lowe in 1592.

Michael and Joane were a married couple – or at least they were reputed to be a married couple around Headington and Cowley. In fact the parish register of Cuddesdon for 5 May 1587 bears this out, but no one seems to have thought to look at that; when Edmund Davis of Wheatley was asked if they were married he said that he believed they were man and wife, and when asked why he believed this he replied that he'd seen them in bed together. Which in view of what was subsequently revealed doesn't seem to prove very much.

Five years after their marriage, the Lowes were at daggers drawn – literally. Henry Messenger dropped in to have a word with Michael one day, but found only Joane at home. 'He's not here', she said. 'He's off among his drabs or his queans', meaning at the very least women of questionable virtue, and quite possibly professional prostitutes. Joane wasn't taking well to this. 'I was once in a mind to have taken a knife and cut his throat', she mused. Trying to pour oil on the waters, Messenger gallantly replied that he couldn't see why Michael had any need to consort with that sort of woman, but Joane was warming to her theme:

> *I considered with myself that if I had cut his throat I should have been hanged for it afterwards. So then I was minded to have taken a couple of knives with me to bed, and when Michael was asleep to have gouged out his eyes....*

'For pity's sake!' said Henry, not liking the direction in which this was going. 'How could you, he being your husband?' 'Yes, I was minded to do it', she repeated.

A view of Old Headington, much as the Lowes would have known it.

When Michael came home and started on his meal, she said to him rather cryptically, 'Thou have as well eat thy meat as to meddle with Samuel.' Samuel was the servant of Mr Curzon their neighbour, and by all accounts not the sort of person one wished to meet in a dark alleyway, but Joane seemed to have the art of controlling him.

The implied threat had its effect on Michael, who shortly afterwards moved his bed out to his father's house, presumably to get a night's sleep without having to wonder if he would have any eyes to open in the morning. Unfortunately he took the best bed, which didn't go down well with his wife.

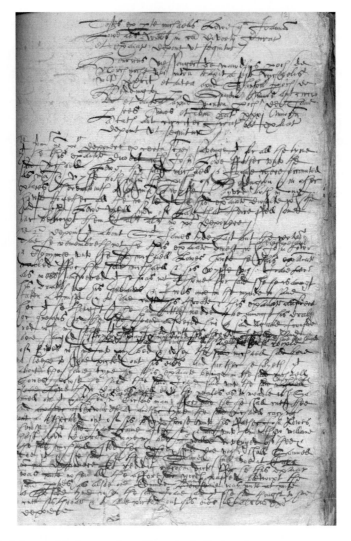

Minded to cut his throat – the evidence in the Lowe case.

'Thou villain!' she screamed at him. 'Thou hast carried away my feather bed out of my house. Thou shall be cut up as small as flesh for the pot.' Oh yes, said Michael, and who exactly is going to do that then? 'Samuel, Mr Curzon's man', she replied. 'I care not by what means I shall be rid of thee.' Michael decided to stay away.

So far one has some sympathy with Michael; maybe his wife drove him to the queans and drabs. But then the perspective shifts. John Bostall, the constable of Headington, received a warrant from the justice Cromwell Lee to arrest Michael on a charge of raping Joane's maid. But privately Joane told Bostall that the rape charge was a ploy: 'He hath beaten me and hath used me very hardly, which causeth me to do this that I do.' Humfrey Sharp of St Clement's Oxford also testified to this:

> *She said she was the only cause that her maid came unto Mr Cromwell Lee for a warrant to arrest her husband of felony for committing a rape, and the reason why she did it was to bridle her husband, for he had beaten her somewhat before.*

After the court case, Stephen Clarke ran across the pair in St Clements, apparently getting on well together for a change, and he said, 'I am glad to see you go so lovingly together.'

'I thank God I am released from one matter,' said Michael, 'and I may thank my wife for th'other. For she was the cause of that, otherwise I had been dispatched from all matters.'

'Why,' Joan interrupted, 'thou didst beat me and misuse me, and I could then have found it in my heart to have killed thee. For I had no other means to keep thee under but to bind thee to the peace and to complain at the assizes, but that which I said was an untruth.'

Obviously, straightforward marital violence was not enough for a wife to lodge a complaint; to get the court to take notice she had to invent a charge which carried some sort of penalty. A man who dealt with a sharp-tongued wife in his own way would be thought none the less of by his neighbours. Humfrey Sharp, who knew about the beating, said that if he had such a wife he would set her upon an island and bid the devil fetch her.

And in an era when keeping one's wife in line by physical violence was the norm, things could easily get out of hand. The classic example of this is the case of Francis and Lettice Staniford in the 1650s, when Francis's hatred of his wife turned into a litany of savage attacks, some of which were clearly attempted murder:

He did take a sword and run it freely at Lettice, saying he would kill her, but missing her body he ran it through her clothes with that force that he stuck it in the wainscot. He did throw a pair of tailor's shears at her and, missing her narrowly, stuck them in a post that was behind her. He did run fiercely at her with a spit, and took up an andiron and hit Lettice in the face with it, and wounded her so that it caused her to lie under the surgeon's hand a long time. He did throw her down stairs when she was big with child, and afterwards he went and trod on her.

Lettice was lucky in being able to escape back to her parents' home, though Staniford took the family to court on the interesting charge that they were depriving him of his conjugal rights. Which says something about the rights he felt he had over his wife.

In an era of refuges for battered wives, offset by the knowledge of how many battered wives never reach them, it should not be forgotten that in previous centuries not only was it difficult to free oneself from a marriage, but a level of casual domestic violence was regarded by many as perfectly natural. At least the Lowes found the way out of their difficulties with a judicial separation, and were able to conduct themselves in a civilized manner at least part of the time. And it wasn't only the poorer families who suffered; in 1560 it was Amy Robsart, wife of Robert Dudley later Earl of Leicester, who was found at the foot of the staircase at Cumnor Place, three miles from Oxford, with her neck broken....

CHAPTER 11

Lock up your children! – The Baby-Eating Pig of Oxford 1300

Anyone who has been kept awake by their neighbour's dog barking, or has seen their prize flowerbed turned to very different purposes by next door's cat, might take comfort from the fact that these are relatively innocent domestic animals. The modern era sees a fairly strong distinction between a residential area and a farm, a distinction which would have been meaningless to anyone in the mediaeval period.

In thirteenth-century Oxford, houses doubled as stables, chickens roamed freely in the streets, and plenty of back yards contained a pig. No one popped down to the supermarket or even the butcher for their meat; everything was home-grown and free-range, and that was where the problems began. The main ones tended to concern bulls; violent animals when

Medieval pigs were not sweet little pink porkers – they were rough, vicious beasts, well used to scavenging and half wild.

roused, these spent a fair amount of time doing damage to other people's property and plenty of compensation cases were brought before the courts. But at least bulls were herbivores; they didn't have a taste for meat. Pigs had a taste for anything, up to and including human flesh.

In July 1300, Matilda Seburgh of Binsey went to visit her mother, Sexburga Spende, taking her son John with her. He was still little more than a baby, nine months old, and sleeping much of the time. It might be tempting to assume that she brought him because she didn't want to leave a small child unprotected at home alone, but the mediaeval mind didn't work in the same way as ours; with the jobs to be done for simple survival, caring for children just had to be fitted in among a hundred other problems. Neighbours helped one another out; if a child was heard crying, anyone hearing it would go to investigate, and would expect you to do the same for them. If Matilda didn't leave her child at home alone, she had no problems with leaving it alone in her mother's house.

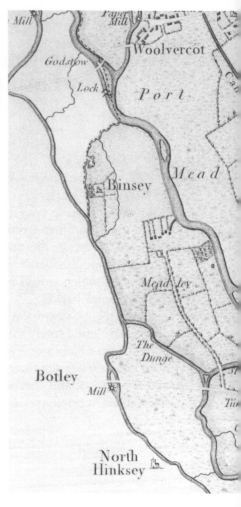

The little village of Binsey on the outskirts of Oxford, from which the pig's victim came.

It was the harvesting season, and Matilda agreed to help her mother out in the fields. The two women left John asleep in his cradle, but one or other of them failed to close the door of the house firmly enough. Animals roamed the streets, and in this case one of them was a neighbouring pig. It succeeded in nosing the door open and forcing its way into the house. While it was unlikely that a pig would attack an adult human being, or even a mobile child, a sleeping baby was a sitting target.

When the two women returned from the field, they were greeted by an appalling sight. The whole of the left side of John's face was missing, together with his left ear; then, perhaps fancying a change of diet, the pig had moved across and eaten the child's right hand. Mercifully he was dead.

Who was to blame? Matilda and Sexburga for not closing the door properly and leaving a child unprotected? The pig's owner for allowing his animal to roam the streets? Such questions fail to take into account the way animals were seen in the thirteenth century.

Any living creature was deemed to be an entity in law. No distinction was made between a man and an animal. You could make a contract with an animal in just the same way as with your neighbour, and what's more call the animal to court if it failed to uphold its side of the bargain. The Church Courts were particularly involved in this, as they could excommunicate criminals whose names were not known and hence who could not be brought to conventional courts under common law. But animals had rights too. At Lausanne in 1478 a group of caterpillars was brought to court for damaging crops. The defence was put forward, as so often, that God had explicitly given animals the right to take food from the world in which they found themselves, and hence the caterpillars were only taking what they had a right to. Ah, said the prosecution, but do they have a right? These are caterpillars. Where, in Genesis, does it say there were caterpillars in Noah's Ark? These are freeloaders without God's permission, and hence should be punished.

The most famous animal trial was probably that of the fieldmice of the Tyrol in 1519. No one tried to claim they hadn't been on board the Ark – they had to come under beasts of the field – but it was still argued that they had no right to destroy crops which had been planted by the labour of human beings. The mice were given a new territory several miles away, and what was more were given safe conduct to it to protect them from cats and other predators. Pregnant mice and

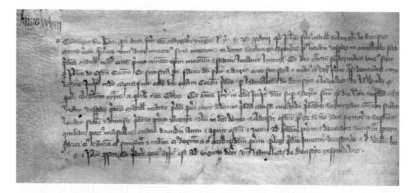

The official coroner's record of the fate of the unfortunate child.

infants were even given a fortnight's respite to prepare themselves for travelling. It may have been a violent age, but in following through principles logically it could sometimes make our own look positively vicious.

What happened to the Oxford pig? Over in Pont de l'Arche in 1408, a pig accused of murder was treated in exactly the same way as a human being would have been; it was shut up in gaol to await trial, and the gaoler received for its maintenance precisely the same sum as he did for each of the men who were locked up with it. Could there have once been a pig locked up in Oxford Castle?

It seems more likely that the murderer received rough justice. In the Coroner's Inquest on the baby, it states that the pig *was* worth twenty pence. The pig appears to have been in the past tense, though there had been no time for a trial. This seems to be much more like our modern reaction to such an incident. And yet it seems a bit rough on the pig's owner, twenty pence was a lot of money; he hadn't left the door unfastened, and that pig was his larder for the coming winter. All the same, would he really have been able to bring himself to eat it?

CHAPTER 12

Robbed by the Milkman – The Story of John Butler 1786

The days before the welfare state were a grim time for those who couldn't support themselves. Prior to the Reformation there were always the monasteries and abbeys to fall back on for charity; it was a Catholic duty to look after the poor, and indeed the chance to do so was valued for the opportunity to buy your way out of purgatory and into heaven earlier. But with the coming of Protestantism and its work ethic matters changed. The poor were equated with the idle; the bogeyman of the prosperous merchant classes became the sturdy beggar, and in times of economic depression when many were thrown out of work, gangs of such beggars roamed the countryside striking fear into the hearts of those who feared for their possessions or even their lives.

It was to combat the growth of the vagrant poor that the concept of imprisonment as a punishment began to evolve; in the early modern period prison was simply somewhere to hold the accused until they could be brought to trial, whereas punishment was something far more visible and (generally) violent, from branding to execution. Imprisonment was the prerogative of debtors, who were not being held in gaol as a punishment but rather to prevent their absconding before they'd paid off their creditors. This idea of holding someone in gaol to keep them from the possible harm they might do in the outside world, rather than as a punishment for harm done, spread to anyone the authorities wanted to keep off the streets, and inevitably to the able-bodied poor.

Of course, no one thought the poor should be treated like debtors; many debtors were gentlemen, and in times of economic uncertainty could end up being those who had been sitting in judgement last week. For the poor, a different kind of imprisonment was devised – one of hard labour and, in the nineteenth century, the treadmill. Even the poor who kept on the outside of the prison walls had nothing to congratulate themselves with; the Elizabethan poor law settlement enabled them to keep body and soul together but little more, while by the later seventeenth century the workhouse had made its appearance, with conditions which often differed little from the gaol.

It was against this background that John Butler, milkman to the University, began his reign of what was intended to be terror, but somehow ended up rather differently. Butler was an honest man, which is always a bad start when planning a career of crime; it means your heart's not in it. He was 45 in 1786, sold milk on the streets of Oxford and supplied many of the colleges. He was also deeply in debt with no immediate likelihood of solvency, and so eventually decided that his only way out of the red was to put on a mask and waylay travellers on the highway – one might call him a highwayman, were it not for the fact that he was so deeply in debt he couldn't afford a horse. When he called for people to stand and deliver, he was the one doing the standing.

His inauspicious career opened on 26 September 1786, on the roadside between Kingston Inn and Buckland, where he stood waiting for his victim with a short gun carried wrapped up in a sack. Others robbed the mail coaches, but then they had horses; Butler had no horse so he robbed the mail boy. This wasn't quite the same thing, as he discovered; mail coaches carry money, but robbing the mail boy was a little like sticking up the deliverer of your daily paper. Butler demanded the money the boy was carrying. But I don't carry money, said the boy. I only carry papers and letters. Oh, I don't know anything about papers, replied Butler. You'd better go on your way. And so the mail boy continued on his rounds, possibly wondering if 1 April had come along late this year.

The next night Butler decided to change his pitch. He set up near Puzey Furze in Berkshire, and at about eight o'clock a certain Mr Andrews came along on horseback. Butler flagged him down and ordered him to stop, but whether he thought

Andrews hadn't heard him, or whether he just wasn't taking chances with a man on a much better form of transport than he possessed, he then fired on him almost immediately from a distance of eight yards. And missed.

Well, not entirely missed; Andrews got a few pellets of duck shot in his arm, and a bit was picked out of his clothing later, but it wasn't enough to slow him down. While Butler was trying to reload, Andrews rode off into the distance, and the Masked Milkman was cheated of another victim.

The following day, Butler refined his methods. Obviously it was a mistake to accost his victims after nightfall, when the light was too bad for him to shoot straight. There was also that question of whether Andrews had in fact heard his request to halt and hand over his valuables; something noticeable which his victims couldn't ignore was obviously called for. He had the very thing.

And so at four in the afternoon on 28 September, Samuel Randall was making his way on horseback over Eynsham Hill when he had a most unusual encounter. What appeared to be a mobile scarecrow came walking up to him in the middle of the road, pointing a large gun in his direction. It then blew a large dog whistle at him, after which it announced, 'Master, I must have your money.' Randall simply didn't believe it; footpads and highwaymen just didn't look like that. 'What do you mean, man?' he asked. Then, on observing that if the scarecrow didn't look the business the gun certainly did, he threw himself on the neck of his horse and dug his spurs into its sides. Butler shot him at point blank range. The gun failed to go off.

By now it was obvious that whatever his qualities as a milkman, Butler didn't have what it takes to be a criminal. He cocked his gun again and fired after Randall, lodging several pieces of shot in the horse's hindquarters; but it was a valedictory gesture. When the authorities came for him, his lawless career had netted him precisely nothing. This cut no ice with the magistrates, who regarded intent and success as much the same thing, and promptly strung him up.

Somehow it seems a bit unfair. Butler was obviously penitent in the gaol, and it was generally agreed he'd been

The milkman meets his end.

driven to what he did by the desperation of his circumstances. On the other hand, one might see it slightly differently if one were Andrews or Randall; they weren't to know they had Oxfordshire's most incompetent footpad facing them. But it was certainly a salutary lesson for those tempted to a life of crime. Villainy requires just as much skill as any other profession, and some people just aren't cut out for it.

CHAPTER 13

John Price – Second Time Unlucky 1784

There's no helping some people. Most people, when apprehended and convicted for a crime, can be reckoned to have reached the end of the line. Price, by an astonishing stroke of luck, escaped the consequences of a crime which was actually proved on him, and yet still ended up on the end of a rope.

John Price was born at Issington in Montgomeryshire, into a family which seems to have had no other inclination towards crime; his father was a flax dresser, and his many other children went into honest work. Not so John; although only eighteen when he committed his crimes in 1784 he looked older, being tall and well built. This made him a natural for the army, but the military life was not noticeably well paid, and John decided he could do better than to risk life and limb for a pittance. The best thing about joining a regiment was the bounty paid on first signing up, but of course you could only sign up once. Well, that's what less enterprising men thought.

Price made a career of signing up. He managed to take the oath in three different regiments before someone spotted what was going on and he had to make a run for it. Perjury and desertion; it didn't look good if Price was captured, as eventually he was at Windsor. He was dragged back before his most recent Colonel and was an absolute certainty for a court martial when fate intervened in a way which would be laughed to scorn in a work of fiction.

As his captors marched him into the presence of the Colonel, they became aware that their officer was not alone. Someone was talking with him; a very important someone. To their astonishment they recognized their sovereign, King George III, who was paying an impromptu visit to the regiment. Being George III, and hence not entirely of a conventional cast of mind even when not suffering from his periodic bouts of insanity (or porphyria), he insisted on hearing the charge against Price, and having done so asked that Price be excused punishment. The Colonel had no choice but to comply, and against all the odds Price found himself at liberty.

Unfortunately, George hadn't heard the whole story. He was told about the desertion from that regiment, which was the reason for Price's capture; what he wasn't told, because no one there knew, was about the other two desertions. Price wasn't safe. One day his earlier offences were going to catch up with him, and the chances of the King of England dropping in to save him again were less than negligible. Considering his situation coldly, he decided to put a lot of distance between himself and anyone who might be able to bring a charge against him, deserted once more, and headed off into Oxfordshire.

So it was that on New Year's Eve 1784, he was heading down Feather Bed Lane in Stokenchurch Wood when he fell in company with a lad of sixteen or so, by the name of Thomas Knight. They hitched a lift on a passing wagon and got into conversation, in the course of which Price learned that his companion was coming down to Great Milton, where he lived. Pausing at a pub on the way, they had a meal of bread and cheese and drank together, then as they were setting off once more Price noted that it was getting dark. A dangerous thing, he said; there were a lot of robberies committed round those parts, and it was difficult to be safe after night fell. This disturbed his companion, who had four shillings and sixpence on

John Price's unexpected saviour, King George III, as seen by Gilray.

him (and made the very serious mistake of informing Price to this effect), so Price asked for the loan of his knife to cut himself a stick and give them a means of defence.

Having acquired his companion's weapon and provided himself with an additional one, Price seems to have undergone a sudden fit of conscience; he handed the knife back to Knight and broke the stick he'd cut. But the lure of the money was too strong – he asked for the knife a second time, cut himself a stout cudgel, and just as the pair entered Milton Common turned on the boy and struck him to the ground. Two swift slashes with the knife across his throat, and Price could stand back and breathe easy. He relieved the boy of his money, then just as he was turning to go, to his horror saw the corpse start to clamber to its feet.

Cutting throats is more of a specialized job than Price realized. Murder was not his forte, and he'd managed to miss the jugular or any other vital part. Coming to his senses, he threw himself at his victim and stamped on the boy's head

So close to home – Milton Common, where Thomas Knight was struck down, just short of his home at Great Milton.

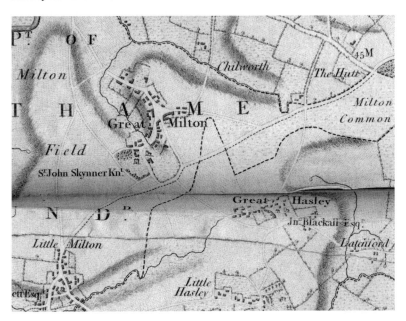

until the body showed no further inclination to get up. Then he ran off in the direction of Tiddington and, noticing that his recent activities had left him with blood-splattered stockings, stole a fresh pair to replace them.

But Thomas Knight was tougher than Price thought. He still wasn't dead, and was able to describe Price and set a hue and cry going. When Price reached Haddenham the next day he discovered rumours were going round about him. He fled to Bicester, but by that time the call was out for his apprehension, and he was sent under guard to Oxford Castle.

At first he showed no regret for his actions, openly wishing that he'd managed to kill the boy, and stating that those who robbed without murdering were fools – which in the state of the law in the later eighteenth century was a fair point, as you were quite likely to hang for either, and at least if you killed your victim there was less chance of a case being made against you. But gradually the slow toil of the legal process wore him down – there was no royal saviour in the wings this time. He was found guilty, sentenced to be executed near the spot where the crime had taken place, and then to be hanged in chains there as a warning to others. It was as he was being measured for the chains that his nerve finally broke, and he made a complete confession of his various crimes.

Verses were circulated which he was said to have wanted published as a warning to others; a remarkable number of criminals seem to have turned poets in their last hours, and there must have been quite a little industry churning out these items and attributing them to particular villains. Still, the John Price stanzas are a nice example of the sort of thing which found its way into print, and can stand in for all the rest:

Young men listen to my story,
Listen virgins young also;
Naught but truth I'll lay before ye,
For I quickly hence must go.

Few my days have been, and evil;
Short and wicked was my life;
(Instigated by the devil)

Full of swearing, fraud and strife.
For which they now will me exhibit
(Alas that I so soon must die!)
Upon an high erected gibbet,
A terror to each passer by.

There for ever I must dangle,
Creaking in the whistling wind,
Where the poor youth I did mangle,
Yet mercy hope in Heav'n to find.

Farewell, Father, farewell, Mother,
Farewell all my kindred dear;
Farewell, sister, farewell, brother –
Pity me when this ye hear.

CHAPTER 14

Kalabergo – The End of the Rope
1851

It would be stretching things much too far to say that the Kalabergo affair was the first Mafia killing in Oxfordshire. Nevertheless, it was a murder which had its origins in Italian jealousy and vengeance, and the need of an individual to flee the country with some urgency to escape a group of people looking for him. On the other hand, it wouldn't be stretching things at all to suggest that the affair changed the administration of criminal justice for all time. And the man who did this could barely speak English.

His name was William Kalabergo, and he was a free and easy individual. A little too free and easy, particularly where the local girls were concerned. In the middle of the nineteenth century, Italian patriarchs imposed a strict code of conduct on their womenfolk, and Kalabergo was intent on breaking it. It didn't matter too much that he was over-fond of a drink; it mattered rather more than he was a bit of a layabout; but his attitude towards the daughters of influential locals was simply not to be tolerated. Eventually he developed a passion for a local girl named Maria, and her family warned him off in no uncertain terms. Kalabergo was young and not inclined to worry about the consequences of his actions. He was heading just the right way for an unfortunate hunting accident in the nearby forest, when his family decided to smuggle him off to safety.

They were lucky in having somewhere they could pack him off to. John Kalabergo, his uncle, had fled Lombardy over three decades earlier to escape conscription under Napoleon, and had ended up in Banbury, where he built up an impressive business as a watch and clock maker. Over the following years he had kept in touch with his family, so when they begged him to give William refuge he grudgingly agreed. His nephew

Butchers Row Banbury, ten years after Kalabergo bought his revolver there.

arrived in England shortly afterwards on a forged passport – his departure was too urgent to go through the business of acquiring a genuine one – and headed for north Oxfordshire.

William Kalabergo was not happy. He'd been torn from the sunny climes of Italy and a personable young lady to be sent to the miserable cold of England where the women were reputed to be rather more reserved with their favours, and the drink of choice was some ghastly stuff called ale instead of wine. Still, gloomy as he was, that was nothing to the gloom exuded by his uncle. John Kalabergo was a respected man in Banbury. He'd got that way by hard work, and the last thing he wanted was to be saddled with some useless parasite out of loyalty to his family. If William was coming to live with him, he was going to mend his ways. John was providing a safe bolt hole; in exchange, he expected the deference due to his seniority and his status.

Two completely different cultures clashed inescapably. John had been formed by the Victorian traditions of hard work and respect for society; William by the Latin love of wine, women

Market Place, Banbury, from which John Kalabergo began his last journey.

and song. John saw William as someone who might one day take over his business; William was only killing time until he could return to Italy. William could hardly believe the conditions which John imposed on him from the very beginning. There was to be no drinking, no gambling, no smoking. Churchgoing with regular communion was imposed. A curfew was put in place; William was to be home by nightfall and was not allowed out again until the next day.

It was a very short time before William began to hate his uncle. His thoughts focused on returning to his family in Italy, to the life which would probably have been terminated quite abruptly if he hadn't left it. Then one day, exasperated beyond measure, John let slip what William hadn't realized. The nephew was expected to take over when John died. Everything was left to him in John's will. And suddenly William saw a way not only of taking revenge on his uncle for the way he was treated, but also of becoming quite rich into the bargain.

The temptation was irresistible, but the practicalities presented some problems. William had very little English and no friends in the country, yet somehow he had to organize and carry out a murder, and leave himself free of suspicion. The problem was increased by his being completely in the dark about how crime detection functioned in this strange land, or what methods and techniques the authorities had at their disposal. This was to be his ultimate downfall, but already he'd shown no aptitude whatsoever for the criminal life.

First of all he needed a weapon. Reckoning that a gun was as safe as anything, on 15 December 1851 he visited a gunsmith on Butcher Row and bought a revolver. Banbury wasn't the smallest town in Oxfordshire, but it wasn't so large

John Kalabergo's shop was in the High Street – shown here ten years after his death in 1851.

that William Kalabergo didn't stand out like a sore thumb. Swarthy, Italianate, with poor English and an accent which made what little he had incomprehensible, everyone knew he was old Kalabergo's worthless nephew. What was he doing buying a gun?

Belatedly William realized this. He took the gun along to another Banbury dealer, Hollands, and exchanged it for a different one, evidently believing that this would cover his tracks. Far from doing so, it simply doubled the number of gunsmiths who could bring evidence against him.

Then there was the problem of the bullets. No one sold bullets in the 1850s; what they sold was a bullet mould, which the would-be murderer had to manipulate with metal, percussion caps, and other paraphernalia to create his own. In practical terms this meant that there was no such thing as a mass-produced bullet. If today's forensic techniques enable the police to determine which gun has fired a particular bullet by the rifling marks, the situation a century and a half ago enabled the very bullet to be traced back to the man who made it. The only safeguard against this was to dispose of the bullet mould in such a way as to ensure it could never be traced back to you. William Kalabergo hid it in the loft of the stables behind his uncle's shop.

He had the motive and had created the means; all that was lacking was the opportunity. This arose shortly after Christmas. To shoot John in his own shop would be asking for trouble. But like many small manufacturers, John Kalabergo was in the habit of making regular trips around the neighbourhood to sell his merchandise, and William intended to take advantage of one of these. He would accompany his uncle, wait until they were on some lonely road, then kill the old man and claim it had been done by footpads.

From the beginning, everything went against him. He could hardly believe how many people around Banbury his uncle knew, or how many of them crossed their path on that trip. Ideally he would have claimed that his uncle had gone on his commercial journey alone, but in a very short time it was obvious he would have to admit to being present. Someone of cooler blood would have postponed his plans, but William was used to acting on impulse. He'd sort it out somehow. Struggling with the loaded cart up Williamscote Hill, he decided the time had come. He slipped the gun out of his pocket, and shot John Kalabergo in the back of the head.

Standing on a lonely road with a cart of timepieces and a dead body, he started to make up his story. Three men had stopped them on the road, demanding money. John Kalabergo, stubborn old fool that he was, had refused. One of the men had pulled out a gun and shot him. He, William, had taken to his heels and run, back in the direction of Banbury, where he would raise a hue and cry and take a party back to find his uncle's body. True to the story, he turned and started to run.

He was half way back to Banbury when he realized he was still carrying the gun which had killed his uncle. He had to get rid of it immediately. Fortunately there were plenty of flooded ditches around, and he flung it into one of them. For reasons no one was ever able to divine, and William never explained, he wrapped his coat around it first. For reasons of panic and carelessness, he forgot about the gunpowder and the exploded percussion cap in his trouser pocket.

Back in Banbury, his first action was to rouse the local Catholic priest, Dr Tandy. Tandy was a good friend of his uncle, and William himself knew the man; he was a logical choice. The story sounded plausible – the roads around Banbury were notoriously lawless, and similar things had happened before. Dr Tandy gathered together a search party and they went out to find John. As soon as they had done so, William's story began to fall to pieces.

John's body was there, where William had said, but so was the cart containing the valuable Kalabergo timepieces. Had a set of thieves deliberately ignored them? Very well, these were intelligent thieves; they had reasoned that there is a limited market for clocks and that they would be advertising their guilt of murder if they attempted to dispose of them. But that didn't explain John Kalabergo's wallet. Crammed with cash from his earlier transactions, it was still in his pocket. A group of thieves who shoot a man for his money then fail to take it when he's dead stretched credulity.

There was also the matter of the wound. William had explained: three men jumped out at them, William put up resistance, they shot him. In the back of the head? At such close quarters that the hair was singed? It made no sense. At least not if it happened the way William claimed.

Once doubt was thrown on William's story, other things started to come out. The purchase of the gun, for example. William claimed he had bought it at the request of old Kalabergo himself – not strictly true, though he had certainly bought it with old Kalabergo's money, stolen from the shop. After all, they were going on a journey around the dangerous roads of north Oxfordshire; they needed protection. Then why had they not taken the gun with them? Why wasn't it in John Kalabergo's pocket? William could hardly say where it actually was without directly incriminating himself. It was at this point that the contents of his trouser pocket came to light, and William was arrested on suspicion of murder.

Once that happened, it was inevitable that the shop and stables would be searched as a matter of course. William could have hidden the bullet mould better. It took no time at all to match it to the bullet in John's brain, and things began to look very black indeed for the nephew. He was told he would be transferred to Wroxham, as Banbury gaol was hardly suitable for holding a man charged with murder, and he realised that if he was to escape now was the only time to do it.

He was placed in an attic room in the North Arms, handcuffed, with two guards to ensure he didn't escape. Unfortunately the guards could have been more efficient. When he indicated to them that the handcuffs were chafing his wrists they unlocked them, then wandered across the room to chat by themselves leaving William by the window. When they next looked up, he'd got the catch of the window undone and was leaving through it. They grabbed at him, but he slid down the thatch outside and then, presumably not foreseen in his plan, dropped like a stone to the pavement below.

It wasn't very difficult for the guards to catch him; no one runs fast with a broken leg. A visiting surgeon diagnosed a fracture of a small bone in his right leg and another in his left arm. When William Kalabergo appeared in court he was

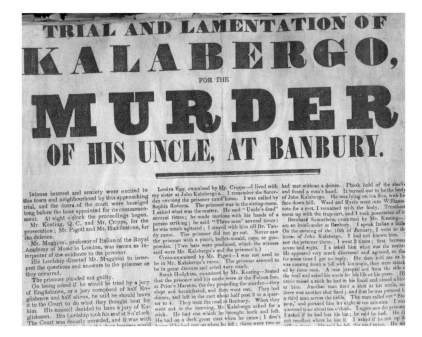

The broadsheet published detailing Kalabergo's crime.

trussed up in splints, which made him appear an even more pitiable figure than he already was.

There seemed very little doubt of the boy's guilt, but the prosecution were still not entirely sure of their case. Much of their evidence was circumstantial – damningly so, but affording the defence possible loopholes. What they really needed was the gun they believed had fired the shot, which they could then show to be the one William bought from Hollands. Clearly he must have dropped it between Williamscote Hill and Banbury, but much of the area was flooded, and a search could take months. Then someone had a bright idea; if all the local mills were to let down their sluices, the excess water would drain away. The result was better than they could have hoped. They not only found the gun. They found it wrapped in William Kalabergo's coat.

One of William's problems – shared by the authorities – was his extremely limited English. It is difficult to try someone if they clearly cannot understand any of the charges you are bringing against them. The Assizes applied to the Home Office for the services of a translator who could understand Kalabergo's obscure Italian dialect. The Home Office replied that any foreigner committing murder in England was expected to find his own interpreter. This rather summed up the prevailing attitude towards William Kalabergo, and he was found guilty of murder.

At first the boy seemed untroubled by the verdict, but while walking in the airing yard of the prison a few days later he suddenly scrambled on to the prison wall with no indication that his broken leg had ever existed, and started to run along it through the vicious spikes which lined the top. From there he leaped on to a steep slated roof, and reached a height of thirty feet above the ground, well out of anyone's reach. The prison guards were in no doubt; Kalabergo was going to kill himself and cheat the hangman.

Sketch of William Kalabergo.

Yet after wandering around the roof and seeing there was no way down, the prisoner sat by a chimney stack and motioned for a ladder to be brought to him. He calmly returned to the ground, and was immediately seized and bundled off to his cell, where he was manacled in irons. It was at this point that his attitude changed. He asked to see Dr Tandy, and through an interpreter held long discussions with him about the crime and the state of his immortal soul. Tandy realized the boy was now terrified, and did his best to comfort him; by an irony he was feeling sympathy for the man who'd killed one of his closest friends. It wasn't his idea of an enjoyable task, but he determined to stand by William through to the gallows.

On the morning of the execution, between 8,000 and 10,000 people crowded around Oxford Gaol and spilled into New Road, eager to see the hanging. Tandy was sickened; he'd come to understand the boy as a frightened human being, and was disgusted by the bloodlust of people who saw his death as an entertainment. When the execution was over, he went to see the governor. The next few minutes were instrumental in changing the nature of executions for ever.

Kalabergo was the last man to be hanged publicly in Oxford.

He expressed his feelings to Robins, the governor, in no uncertain terms. He drew parallels with the women who sat knitting at the foot of the guillotine in revolutionary France. He condemned public executions as barbaric, and said they must end. And Robins agreed with him.

Nothing happens overnight, but William Kalabergo's was the last public execution carried out in Oxfordshire, and one of the last anywhere. The tide was turning. Plenty of people resented the loss of this enjoyable entertainment, but those in authority could see that a society in which the death of a living creature was seen as fun for the spectators had no claim to be called civilized. Tandy's words helped tip the scales. So finally William Kalabergo, womaniser, layabout, and murderer, did some good – more than he could ever have imagined. The pity was, he was never to know it.

CHAPTER 15

Jenny Bunting's Parlour – What Is a Record Office *for*?
Eighteenth Century

A madwoman running screaming through an old quarry at dead of night – is this real or an old Stephen King draft? And is it true that if you read it in the record office it must have really happened? Or could it be just as much fiction as the master of horror?

Out beyond the old rifle butts at Hinksey, just to the south of Oxford, there is an overgrown quarry known as Jenny Bunting's Parlour. There are no official records of the quarry or its sinister inhabitant, but one set of volumes in the Oxfordshire Record Office gives the origin of the place's peculiar name. These are the manuscript books of Thomas Symonds, known as the Eynsham Antiquary, and the point at which the dedication of the record office to truth and accuracy shades over into report and hearsay.

Most counties have a Symonds – a man who has dedicated his life to picking up and writing down local tales, old stories, and eyewitness accounts of events long ago. Symonds was even more dedicated than most; his day job was being rector of Eynsham, and as an educated man he copied down old documents which came his way, many of which have never been seen again. The nine manuscript books he left behind, bound in crumbling red leather – fragments of it cover the keyboard as I write – contain hundreds of stories and scraps of information found nowhere else.

Do we believe them? As scholars and archivists, of course we have to be suspicious: no reason to think he's trying to fool us, but no proof he isn't either. And yet stories where there is an alternative and trustworthy source suggest he can be fairly accurate, and some of the stories do make a lot of sense.

Qualified acceptance then. There's no other reason I know of for a disused quarry acquiring such a peculiar nickname.

Peggy Broadway was born in Yarnton in the later seventeenth century. Her father wasn't the most law-abiding individual, but it wasn't until she was fifteen years old and her only brother five that he decided to make the move which would gain him riches and six feet of Dorset earth. A widower, he took his son Edward to live with him on the south coast, while setting his daughter up in service with Thomas Clayton, the warden of Merton College. As soon as possible he packed Edward off to a respectable school in Southampton, thereby leaving himself unencumbered to pursue his chosen profession – that of smuggler.

And he was remarkably successful at the job. He quickly went into partnership with a man named George Mytton, and between them they provided a real-life counterpart of the fictional Dr Syn – respectable and respected gentlemen by day, ruthless gangsters by night. Their wealth grew by leaps and bounds, but as so often happens they pushed their luck a little too far, and during one of their operations engaged a

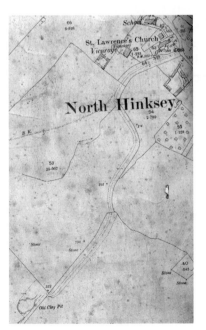

well-armed French ship in battle. Mytton was killed outright and Broadway seriously wounded. He made his way, dying, back to his home, and called his son to hear his deathbed confession.

If Edward was surprised to learn what had been paying his school fees all those years, he was astonished to learn he had a sister – leaving Oxford at the age of five, he had only the vaguest recollections of her. Broadway explained that he had written to the girl

A map of North Hinksey, showing the clay pit where Jenny Bunting died.

several times but received no reply – now he wanted to provide for her. He made his ill-gotten gains over to Edward and told him to find his sister.

Shortly after his father's funeral, Edward visited Oxford, but could find no trace of Peggy. Thomas Clayton had died in 1693, years earlier, and no one knew what had become of his servants. Eventually Edward used some of his inheritance to buy a house at Wootton, and settled down there in peace and quiet, until he started to hear some very odd stories.

Servants talked of a strange woman who wandered on Wootton Heath and had supernatural powers. She was seen talking to herself in a peculiar way, making wild gestures and causing the superstitious locals to give her a wide berth. Her name was Jenny Bunting. Edward started to take an interest in the woman. Of course he was an educated man, a man of the world; he had no time for old wives' tales. The woman was clearly mad, nothing more. And yet....

One evening, driven by curiosity, he slipped out of the house and went looking for the woman. He soon found her, muttering incoherently to herself, flinging her arms about, and after watching for a while decided to speak to her. What he hadn't taken into account was that no one spoke to Jenny Bunting. The locals avoided her with superstitious terror. On hearing his voice she screamed and ran, and he instinctively followed her. When he finally caught up with her it was in an overgrown quarry, where she lay unconscious with fright and exhaustion. He brought her round, but it was soon obvious that in her weakened condition she had received a fatal shock, and would not even allow him to send for a doctor. Instead she asked him to hear her confession, and for the second time he found himself at a deathbed hearing something he would much rather not have known.

Jenny lived by selling odds and ends on the streets of Oxford – there were many like her.

Her true name, she told him, was Peggy Broadway. She had been put in service with Dr Clayton when her father and young brother left the district, but after a short time had fallen in with a man who promised to marry her. It was an old line, but it worked once again. On this occasion he wanted her to travel to Yorkshire with him, where he lived, but unfortunately they needed money for the journey. The only available source of this was Thomas Clayton, and so she was persuaded to rob her master and flee his house at dead of night.

Needless to say, her lover was interested in Yorkshire and the money, but rather less in Peggy. Having got his hands on the valuables she'd stolen he deserted her, leaving her alone and penniless as the authorities tried to track her down. By sheer good luck, she fell in with a gang of gypsies and told them her story; they took pity on her and carried her with them, shielding her from any enquiries being made by Clayton. For many years she travelled with them, and when they finally parted company she was able to maintain herself as a pedlar.

Eventually, however, she found her way back to Oxford and stumbled over the disused quarry, hidden by overgrown bushes. Thinking that it would give her a safe haven, she thatched it over roughly and had lived there ever since, supporting herself by selling clothes pegs, cabbage nets, and other small items on the streets of Oxford. The strain of the life gradually affected her mind, and she started using wild gestures and muttering to herself, which gave her the reputation of a latter-day witch and the nickname Jenny Bunting.

And so Edward Broadway had to live not only with the knowledge that his father was a notorious smuggler, but with the realization that he had accidentally killed his own sister. The story is a little too neat – classic tragedy – and yet far from implausible. Plenty of young girls were seduced into a life of crime by men promising to marry them in an era when a woman had little chance in life without a male protector. A good number of fortunes were based on activities which wouldn't bear too close a scrutiny. How far folk myth has tinkered with this particular story we will never know, but as a scenario for late-seventeenth-century Oxford it works well enough.

In the final analysis a record office is for maintaining the truth, insofar as that slippery commodity can be pinned down. But just occasionally it can be for maintaining a flavour of the times as well. Provided one isn't seduced into believing that the story of Jenny Bunting is absolutely accurate, her domestic tragedy can tell us more about the misery of betrayal and greed 300 years ago than a whole book of statistics.

Chapter 16

Fisticuffs – Disturbing the Peace with Riot, Rout, Assault and Murder
1817

We'd call it boxing; the nineteenth century called it prize-fighting, and the Romans called it *pugilatus.* Given the level of violence endemic in earlier centuries in England, it may seem odd that so many determined attempts were made to stamp it out, but then prize-fighting was a dangerous sport. No gloves but bare knuckles, and no time limits. Basically it consisted of two men trying to beat one another insensible for the delectation of the crowd, and generally to win a fair number of bets into the bargain.

The attitude of the authorities was ambiguous. Broughton's Amphitheatre was built behind Oxford Road in London as early as 1742 to house the activity, and from the 1790s there are well-attested boxing schools around the country.

The noble art of 160-round matches, which sometimes left one participant dead.

Following the pugilists became a mark of the sporting gentry, as was shown by the sort of money changing hands. In 1824 Tom Winter, a favourite fighter nicknamed 'Spring', beat Langan for £1,000. John Gully, a former butcher, acquired so much wealth as a prize-fighter that he was able to become MP for Pontefract in 1835.

But where serious violence was being done, the forces of law and order stepped in. Tom King beat Heenan nearly to death in 1863, and both were brought to court; they were given a conditional discharge on promising not to offend again. Four years later a much anticipated contest for the championship between Mace and the giant O'Baldwin hit a stumbling block when Mace was arrested. The following year railways were prohibited from carrying people travelling to a prize-fight, though how anyone proved it is open to question.

This was the background against which the Oxfordshire magistrates determined to put a stop to public prize-fighting in the county. The event which brought this to a head was the fight between William Gill and George Norley for what was described as the Championship of the Lightweights, the stakes being £250 a side. Eynsham, a few miles to the west of Oxford, was a favourite spot for prize-fighting, as it lay right by the river dividing Oxfordshire from Berkshire; any sign of trouble from the parish constables and the entire party decamped across the river out of their jurisdiction, being careful to commit no breach of the peace in Berkshire territory. It also contained a reasonable number of sporting gentlemen of the better class who encouraged the parties, and who provided 'influence and intimidation' to ensure that no steps were taken against them. But this time they were up against the big guns.

In 1846 Eynsham had a new vicar who was prepared to stand up to the vested interests. Early on the morning of 12 May he learned of the proposed fight and immediately rode over to Oxford and obtained warrants for the arrest of the two participants from Thomas Lucas, the City Marshall. The prize-fighters and their friends duly assembled in Eynsham, the contestants being weighed in, when someone noticed that among the crowd were Lucas and three of his assistants.

Eynsham as it is today.

Immediately they upped sticks and moved to Northleigh, four miles away, where a ring was formed and discussions put under way on the appointment of the referee. The discussions became rather heated, and by the time a compromise had been agreed, the promoters became aware that the crowd of spectators had been swollen by the addition of a contingent of policemen. Once again, they took down the ring and headed out into the countryside to Whitty Green, three miles further on, and bordering Wychwood Forest at Ramsden Heath.

This time they were undisturbed, and the fight started at three o'clock, lasting until after seven and consisting of 160 rounds. As many as 3,000 people were present, many of whom came in a variety of vehicles; since the fight took place only thirty yards from the Witney to Chipping Norton Turnpike Road, the road was effectively closed down. Gill was declared the winner when it became obvious that Norley was not going to last much longer. The subsequent indictment against Gill said that he 'did unlawfully, riotously and routously make an assault on George Norley and did beat, wound and ill-treat him so that his life was despaired of'. Norley seemed to be getting the worst of it, one spectator laconically observed, which probably explained why he had to be carried back to Eynsham and put to bed at the Swan Inn.

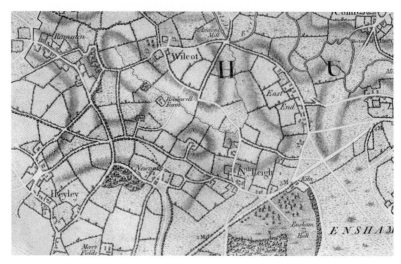

From Eynsham to North Leigh to Ramsden Heath – the route of the retreating prizefighters.

It was at this point that it became clear why Lucas and the police hadn't bothered to follow the fight out to Ramsden Heath and shut it down. No matter how often they prevented a fight, the promoters would simply set up another. Their plan was to let the fight happen, let the participants kill one another if they had a mind to, then mop up everyone involved afterwards when they had something to charge them with. Norley was easy; he could barely walk, let alone run away. All they had to do was stroll into his room at the Swan and tell him he was under arrest.

This probably explains why they weren't paying sufficient attention. Lucas sent two constables in to carry out the arrest and sit with the groaning man until he could be taken into custody. The last thing they were expecting was a mob-handed rescue.

As the constables sat by the bed they heard the sudden thundering of feet on the stairs, then the door of the room crashed open and a dozen ruffians burst in; instantly they blew the candles out so that the constables couldn't see their faces, grabbed Norley and put him in a blanket, carried him downstairs into a waiting chaise, and rushed him off to Oxford where he was put on the next train to London. The Oxfordshire police never saw him again.

The Swan Inn, Eynsham, where George Norley was dragged out of bed by the law.

Still, they got Gill. The man fought, but 160 rounds tends to take it out of one and he was no match for the strong arm of the law. He ended up with three weeks imprisonment, and was bound over in £100 to keep the peace.

What they didn't get was the sporting gentlemen. Bribery and intimidation did their work, and no one could be found to give evidence against them. Lucas and his men hadn't been present at the actual fight, and so could give no evidence in their own right. Even the indictment against Joseph Batts, an ostler at the Swan Inn, for organizing the rescue of Norley had to be dropped for lack of evidence.

Why were the authorities so determined to put a stop to prize-fighting in the county? The answer lay thirty years back, in the Batts–Claydon contest of 1817 at Radley Common. On 28 April the two contestants met in a match which lasted a mere three-quarters of an hour. From the start it was evident that Claydon had the upper hand. In the first round he placed a hit to his opponent's head which floored him and drew blood. A trial of strength in the second round saw him throw Batts, and high odds were frantically offered on him without finding any takers. In the third round he closed up one of Batts' eyes, and a lancet had to be applied to allow Batts to continue. So matters continued until the tenth round, when suddenly Claydon started to go to pieces. By the fourteenth round he was on his knees, and according to a commentator, 'Batts got his head under his left arm and made his head as frightful as his own. After tiring himself with hitting, he let loose of him to go down.' From there on it was a slow collapse, and 'in the twenty seventh round Batts gave him his death blow on the jugular vein.'

A flamboyant piece of sporting journalist's prose; unfortunately it proved to be all too accurate. To his horror, Batts discovered that he had actually killed Claydon. The ring was flooded with medical men, but there was nothing they could do; Claydon died without regaining consciousness. Tongues began to wag. Was it not suspicious, some said, that after starting out so well Claydon suddenly lost co-ordination and started to flag? Wasn't it true that there was a lot of powerful money wagered on Batts? Just what was in the refreshments that Claydon was offered between rounds? The word *laudanum* was mentioned, and soon began to buzz around the spectators. Had Claydon been drugged to ensure a victory for Batts?

Cooke, the City Coroner, had no choice but to order an autopsy on Claydon's body. He opened the stomach, but found nothing out of the ordinary; Batts, he said, had won the fight fair and square. But by now the tide of opinion was turning well against the victor. After all, he was a professional pugilist; Claydon was something else altogether.

'Claydon', said a contemporary broadsheet writer,

> *was a labourer and lived at Weston-on-the-Green, about eight miles from Oxford; he has ever borne an excellent character; he was honest sober and industrious; kept an aged mother from the necessity of applying to the parish for relief; assisted other relatives; and was esteemed and beloved by his neighbours.*

So what was this evident paragon of all the virtues doing attempting to beat the famous William Batts of Witney to a pulp?

> *Claydon had one ingredient in his composition which unfortunately caught the attention of a certain set of persons – he was truly courageous – he was also gifted with considerable bodily strength; he never sought a quarrel for he was always deemed an*

harmless and inoffensive man, yet he was too courageous to brook an insult. Simple and uneducated, his feelings were easily worked on by those who are always seeking for amusement, without reflecting that what is sport for them may be death to others.

Such men as these dragged him into two or three previous battles, and enjoyed the supreme satisfaction of boasting that they gained their bets! He, of course, attracted the attention of the prize fighters; of those who make a trade of boxing, whose loss would create no great chasm in society. Thus beset by betting men and boxers, he entered into an agreement to fight Batts, not for the gratification of any feelings of his own, but for the amusement of others! He had been repeatedly heard to declare that he had no wish to fight, that he did not know why he fought, but that he would not refuse a challenge.

For a broadsheet writer, mindful as any contemporary journalist of the need to chime in with the prejudices of his readers, to state the case against prize-fighting that baldly suggests a strong current running against the practice. For all his evident innocence of shady practice, Batts was indicted on a charge of wilful murder and the jury took no more than half an hour to send him to answer at the Assizes. In all honesty his crime could be considered no worse than manslaughter, and he was given six months imprisonment.

With such a following wind, it was hardly surprising that the Oxfordshire magistrates were determined to stamp out prize-fighting once and for all, and that they had a particular determination to catch the promoters of the practice. Let the broadsheet writer have the last word:

We trust that our neighbourhood will not again be disgraced by an exhibition of this nature, that men will no longer be brought together to bruise and maim one another for the gratification of those who pride themselves in encouraging a science, which by all thinking persons is considered grossly immoral and calculated to bring disgrace on the promoters of it and misery on those whom they patronize. To those who still feel inclined to encourage it, we recommend a peep into the cottage of poor Claydon at Weston, where they may behold him stretched out in his coffin, surrounded by his aged destitute mother, and his weeping relatives and neighbours.

CHAPTER 17

Francis Lovell – The Final Disappearing Act
1480–87

The cat, the rat, and Lovell the dog
Ruleth all England under the hog.

I t's not great poetry, but it didn't warrant summary execution; Collingbourne is said to have been condemned for writing those lines about Richard III and his ministers. The hog was the boar, Richard's own crest, while the first two creatures were Sir William Catesby and Sir Richard Ratcliffe. The dog was part of Lovell's heraldic symbolism, though the sarcastic implication of a fawning creature following at Richard's heels was hard to miss.

The Lovell family were based at Minster Lovell in Oxfordshire, and they had a history of loyalty to their reigning

Minster Lovell, the ancestral home of the Lovell family, now a picturesque ruin.

monarch. Some fifty years before Richard's death, Sir Richard Lovell had married Elizabeth Douglas of Lochleven Castle in Scotland. She was maid of honour to Joanna, Queen of James I of Scotland, and happened to be in the royal apartments when a band of assassins came looking for the King. She ran to secure the room, but found that traitors in the household had already removed the heavy oaken bar which was slotted into the iron brackets on the door to fasten it shut. Immediately she pushed her arm between the brackets to replace it; the arm was shattered as the assassins broke in and finished off the King.

Half a century later, Francis Lovell found that he too would be risking his skin for his King. He was a ward of the Duke of Warwick, in whose household Richard spent some time as a boy; they seem to have formed a close friendship. He served on Richard's expedition to Scotland in 1480, and was created Viscount Lovell early in 1483 by Edward IV, who died that April. On Richard becoming King in June Lovell was made Lord Chamberlain, and was instrumental in putting down Buckingham's rebellion. Two years later Lovell was at Bosworth Field with Richard when the King was defeated by the future Henry VII. At this point he pulled the first of his disappearing acts; when the dead were counted up on the field, Lovell was nowhere to be seen.

In fact, on realizing the day was lost, Lovell had fled to sanctuary at Colchester. He hid there until he was able to organize a Yorkist revolt against Henry, and emerged to lead the troops in Yorkshire. But the revolt was unsuccessful; Henry's partisans crushed it – only on counting up the dead and prisoners, Lovell was again nowhere to be seen.

This time he'd fled to take refuge with Margaret of Burgundy in Flanders. But he was still determined to destroy Henry, and his chance came with the appearance of Lambert Simnel. Simnel was a fraud, tutored by a disenchanted Oxford priest to pretend to be Edward of Warwick, who had a good claim to the English throne; the flaw in the scheme was that Henry VII had the

The notorious Richard III, friend of Lovell, from a stained glass window of 1478. Note the lack of hunched back and withered arm before the Tudor propagandists got to work on him.

real Edward imprisoned in the Tower and was able to prove it. Nevertheless, Lovell joined with John de la Pole, amassed troops in Ireland in the name of the pretended Edward, and invaded England. He met Henry's forces at the battle of Stoke Field in June 1487, and was decisively defeated. Only yet again he pulled one of his famous disappearing acts.

Rumour said he had been killed in the battle, but his corpse was never found. Then reports of witnesses came in that he had been seen on horseback trying to swim the river Trent; the river was in full flood and the witnesses believed he had been swept away and drowned. And yet the name of Lovell would not lie down. It was whispered that he'd got across the river, that he was still alive waiting for his chance to reappear yet again and attack Henry. He was living in a secret chamber at Minster Lovell, the whispers said, cared for by a loyal servant but completely undetectable by anyone searching. Certainly he was never seen, but the threat of his emergence lived on.

And yet the years passed, and Lovell did not appear. Henry died; his son Henry VIII ascended the throne. The Tudors passed, and the Stuarts; the Civil War raged across England; James II was ousted by William of Orange, and the reign of Queen Anne began. Over two centuries had passed since Lovell's last disappearance; he would hardly re-emerge now. But he did.

In 1708, a new chimney was being laid at Minster Lovell. While laying the foundations, the builders broke through what they had assumed was a solid wall and found it was hollow behind. Further investigation proved that they had stumbled on a large, concealed vault. Bringing lights, they and the family made their way through the wall to see if anything lay beyond.

In the middle of the chamber was a table, on which were the remains of a book, pen and paper. Seated in a chair drawn up to the table was the skeleton of a man. Nearby were the mouldering remains of a cap, which could be judged to be in a style of some two centuries ago. Lovell had returned to his ancestral home, but either by accident or betrayal the servant charged to look after him had failed, and left him trapped in the secure haven which had become his tomb. And once again he had returned.

As they watched, the cold outside air flooded into the sealed room and struck the skeleton. Before their eyes it shivered and crumbled into a heap of dust.

Francis Lovell had played his very final disappearing act.

CHAPTER 18

Gentlemen of the Road I –
The One-armed Bandit
1784

The euphemism 'Gentleman of the Road' for highwayman usually has a lot more to do with the lifestyle to which any successful looter of stagecoaches could aspire than with actual social status. On the other hand, it was a quick way of making money for those prepared to take the risks, and hence might be a handy way of replenishing the family fortunes of good families fallen on hard times.

One such family was the Dunsdons of Fullbrook, who lived at the Old Manor House there and just to prove it scratched their name on the glass of one of the windows. Money was getting tight for the old middling families in the later eighteenth century; agriculture didn't pay as it used to, and they had no skills for moving into the new industries. But the Dunsdons did have two useful skills: they were good shots and had no moral conscience whatsoever, which clearly fitted them for a career in the wealth redistribution business.

The three Dunsdon brothers went by the implausible but true names of Richard, Thomas and Henry – Tom, Dick and Harry, and there have been those who claim they invented the

The only means of travelling long distances in the days of the highwaymen – another group of Oxford passengers prepare to take their chances.

phrase – the eldest being Richard, who was born in 1745. In the eighteenth century Wychwood Forest was a happy hunting ground for such men; covering a huge area, it took in several major travelling routes, ensuring a plentiful supply of victims. At first the brothers started small, picking off farmers on their way to market and stealing their stock, which could easily be hidden in the woodland. Slowly their reputation began to grow, and with it the risks.

Typical hotheads, they were as happy being shot at as doing the shooting. One story of the brothers has them splitting up one snowy night to go about their nefarious business, resulting in them actually meeting one another in the middle of a snowstorm coming from opposite directions, two from Northleach and one from Frogmill. Immediately each party opened fire on the other, and Harry's mare had her ear shot off, while Tom got a bullet in his boot. The tracks on the ground must have looked quite interesting too; apparently the Dunsdons used to shoe their horses the wrong way round to confuse any pursuers, leading to a terrible expenditure in horses.

By now they were local notables – sufficiently well-known to be recognized, and sufficiently feared not to be identified if any officer of the law chanced by. They used to drink regularly at the George Inn in Burford and were known for it, but no one was prepared to point them out and risk the consequences.

At any rate, they might have continued as minor villains if it hadn't been for the exploit which lifted them into the legendary class – the attack on the Oxford Mail (the coach, not the newspaper), which netted them close on £500 and made them a power to be reckoned with. Shortly afterwards they discovered that the Wychwood area was too hot to hold them, and opened a second branch of the business in Epping Forest until things had cooled down and they could return.

Unfortunately for them, it was at this point that things started to go wrong. They decided to expand their activities from stopping coaches and mounted a raid on Tangley Manor, a house between Burford and Stow-on-the-Wold. Accounts vary as to whether the owners of the Manor were taken by surprise or had been tipped off and had a reception party waiting, but when Dick put his arm through the suspiciously unsecured shutter in the door to lift the latch on the other side he found it grabbed and held fast. Unable to get free, and with a vivid picture of a gibbet in his mind, he screamed at his brothers, 'Cut it off!', which they duly did, hacking his arm off at the elbow and leaving the Manor's inhabitants with a somewhat grisly trophy of the affair. Tom and Harry managed to get their brother as far as Fifield, where the landlord of the Merry Mouth Inn was known to have some surgical skill, but he refused to help them; the two brothers beat him up and left him for dead, but this was no help to Dick who meanwhile expired, leaving Tom and Harry with that most difficult of encumbrances to account for: a corpse.

The only thing to do was to bury him on the quiet. Thus it was that a local hedger and ditcher, heading out to work at five one morning, had the hair-raising experience of spotting two mounted men heading into Wychwood Forest, leading a horse over which was thrown the corpse of a third. As he followed them, he saw them drag the corpse off its horse and throw it into a shallow grave. Unfortunately it was at this point that he drew attention to himself, so the brothers shot him and threw his body into the grave with Dick before they filled it in.

It might have been expected that the Dunsdons would keep their heads down after that, but in fact they seem to have become worse. Back in the eighteenth century, the Bibury race meeting near Burford was almost as fashionable as Epsom or Newmarket, and was the perfect locale for the brothers to practice their other favourite pastime, gambling. They were well known in the area, but no one was about to inform on a pair of ruthless murderers as long as they could look the other way. After all, they blended in; fashionable dress, almost certainly removed forcibly from the person who'd actually paid for it, and plenty of ready money to flash around.

On Whit Sunday 1784, they joined the gambling party at Capp's Lodge Summer House, and if anyone was uncomfortable with their company, he kept it to himself. The night wore on, and at four in the morning the brothers were still there, risking their money with the best of them. Nasty suspicions were beginning to circulate in the room. Why were they staying so late? Why were they so casual about their losses? Was it possible that they had accomplices outside to waylay any unfortunate gentleman leaving alone, or even to raid the party and carry off everyone's winnings? Might it not be an idea to request them to leave now, while the going was good?

Tom and Harry didn't want to leave. In fact they were quite determined to stay. William Harding, the tapster at Capp's Lodge, a man of far greater courage than common sense, grabbed hold of Harry to eject him forcibly. Harry didn't even waste time being surprised; he just pulled out a loaded pistol and shot Harding at point blank range. He must have been something the worse for drink, as he missed; not entirely, but merely shattering Harding's arm rather than killing him. Harding, a tough individual, continued to hang on. Harry drew a second pistol, and this time he didn't miss; he shot Harding in the chest.

At this point events began to move with some speed. Perkins, an ostler at Capp's Lodge, ran up and kicked Harry's feet from under him before he could produce a third gun. Meanwhile Tom had belatedly noticed what was happening and ran to help his brother, pulling his own loaded guns out of his coat. Perkins snatched up one of Harry's discharged weapons from the floor, and before Tom could fire struck him over the head with it. The landlord threw himself into the fray, and eventually the Dunsdons were captured.

This time they had shot a man in front of witnesses, and it would be difficult to wriggle out of the consequences. In fact Harding was even tougher than many had given him credit for,

The tree from which the highwaymen were hung in chains.

Nineteenth-century artist's impression of Harding's daughter, pointing to the bullet holes in her father's coat.

and lingered on for some months, but eventually he died and the charge was one of murder. Tom and Harry were found guilty and sentenced to be executed, with their bodies to be gibbeted at the scene of their crimes.

Meanwhile Harding's daughter was deeply affected by her father's fate. She took the red plush waistcoat he had been wearing during the fight and altered it so that it fitted her. Thereafter she was seen wandering round Burford, pointing out the holes made by Harry's bullets and attacking the impotence of the forces of law and order which could not protect William. Many years later she could be seen as an old woman, still travelling the streets of the town in the ragged remains of the old coat.

The brothers were hanged in chains on an oak tree in Wychwood Forest. On the bark was cut the legend 'H.D. – T.D. 1784' as a grim memorial. Locals claimed the tree had not grown another inch since that date.

One final irony marked the brothers' passing. After their execution, they were dumped unceremoniously in the back of a cart and the driver instructed to take them to the tree which would hold their remains. It was a warm day, and under the heat of the sun the driver felt that a pint of ale would do him no harm. Passing through Burford he pulled up in front of a convenient inn and called to the landlord for a glass. The inn was the George. The Dunsdons had stopped off for one last pint at their local.

The highwaymen's initials, still carved deep into the bark.
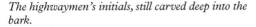

CHAPTER 19

Gentlemen of the Road II – The Royalist Highwayman c. 1642–48

If someone is going to relieve you of your hard-earned money, does it really matter how he does it? Provided he doesn't actually beat you about the head or belabour you with a bicycle chain, would you really care if he was polite? Would it do him any good in court if he'd worked on the 'I say, old boy, awfully sorry but would you mind handing over your wallet?' principle? Oddly enough, back in the seventeenth century, one man found that it did – a certain James Hind, known as a genuine gentleman of the road.

Hind was born in Chipping Norton in 1616, the son of a wealthy saddler who seems to have had great hopes for his intelligent son – at least he had him taught at the local grammar school to a higher level than most saddlers' children would achieve. He then tried to teach him the saddler's trade, but with no success whatsoever – James simply wasn't interested. In desperation his father apprenticed him to a local butcher, but James found that even less to his taste, and eventually ran away down to London. There he got drunk and found himself in the lockup in Poultry, where a meeting took place which set him on to his career.

Among all the low-life of the prison, he saw that one inmate was treated with awe and respect by the rest. This was Thomas Allen, the highwayman, and one of the most powerful figures in the underworld. Hind was fascinated and scraped an

The record of James Hind's baptism from the Chipping Norton parish registers.

acquaintance with the man, who took to the young lad, clearly reckoning that he'd be a good recruit for the Allen gang. He paid Hind's fine for him, and took him back to join one of the most notorious gangs of highwaymen at that time infesting the roads around London.

From the beginning it was obvious that Hind was a highwayman of a different stamp, as different from the old

Woodcut of Captain James Hind himself, the gentleman highwayman.

two-pistols, 'Stand and deliver' brigade as a computer hacker is from a mugger. For a start, although there have been odd cases of females dressing up as men to rob on the highways, Hind was probably unique in dressing up as a woman. Not for fun, but for profit; he'd got his eye on a lecherous old lawyer who was very careful except where women were concerned. In his very impressive disguise Hind was invited back to the lawyer's chambers, where he produced his loaded pistol and cleaned out the lawyer's pockets. He also spotted a strongbox whose contents he fancied; this time he got a real woman to get the lawyer drunk – presumably by now the victim was carrying out simple tests on the local doxies – and pick his

And the record of his marriage in a brief moment when the heat was off.

pockets of the keys. Hind emptied the strongbox, relocked it, and got his accomplice to replace the keys in the lawyer's pocket, thereby accomplishing what must have appeared an impossible crime.

Indeed Hind seems to have led a double life. He married Margaret Rowland in Chipping Norton in 1638, and the couple had four children, but when Hind wasn't being a quiet family man he was roaming the length and breadth of England with Allen's gang, robbing wherever he went. Yet even here, he seems to have broken the mould. The various rhymes and chapbooks detailing his exploits portray him as a sort of Robin Hood, more interested in pulling off a clever coup or a good joke than in the money, and often returning the cash he stole to his victims. Near Wantage he robbed a poor farmer going to buy a cow at market, who begged him not to take the money as it was all he had. Sorry, said Hind, but I'm a bit short right now; meet me here in a week. A week later he gave his victim back double the money he'd stolen.

If it was true that Hind was more interested in excitement than villainy, it explains what happened next. In 1642 the English Civil War broke out, and Hind enlisted the whole of the Allen gang on the King's side. He himself became a member of Compton's Horse, the young Lord Compton hailing from Compton Wynyates only a dozen miles from where Hind grew up. A highwayman was a gift to the Royalist forces; apart from his skill in horsemanship in a war largely based on cavalry charges, Hind had some very unorthodox skills where everyone else was fighting by the book. Cutting off the enemy's support by raiding supply trains was a vital part of warfare, and no one was better at accosting by the roadside than Hind.

He went with Compton to defend Colchester against the Parliamentarian forces, and made a good job of it until Fairfax successfully cut their communication lines and forced the town to surrender in 1648. Compton was captured and imprisoned, but Hind had a long history of slipping out of tight situations. One account says he went back to his old trick of dressing as a woman, another that he disguised himself as a sailor, but either way when Fairfax searched the town there was no sign of James Hind.

Allen's gang were back on the road as highwaymen, but this time it was personal; they were not merely standing outside law and order but against the form of law and order represented by Cromwell's government. They started to target those they believed stood for the regime or who had benefited from the Royalists' loss of their estates. Finally they became too daring and took their activities to their logical conclusion – they planned to hold up Cromwell himself.

The Lord Protector was at Huntingdon; the gang lay in wait on the road leading back into London. They knew he'd be well guarded, but they'd underestimated badly. Cromwell had a major detachment of troops riding with his coach. Although the gang had the advantage of surprise, the troops had the advantage of numbers. What was intended as a swift surgical strike turned into a pitched battle with the highwaymen hemmed in on all sides. Mercilessly they were gunned and hacked down. Finally Allen and some of the others surrendered, although they knew that their next stop would be the gallows at Tyburn. But one man broke through the Parliamentarian forces and rode for his life with the troopers on his heels; Hind escaped once again to fight another day.

Only now he was on his own. Although he'd become a legend, he was still only one man and he had to be careful. In the same way that the figure of Robin Hood was taken up by the minor nobility who felt themselves badly treated by the King, so Hind was taken up by Royalists who resented Cromwell's government. Because of the way he polarized political attitudes, it becomes difficult to say which stories of Hind are true, which exaggerated, and which simply made up. Still, some of Hind's most noted exploits come from this period, and it would be nice to think there was at least a grain of truth in them.

Such as the story of the Worcestershire men in the inn at Oxford. These were local notables, the administrators of a regime that Hind despised, and yet the highwayman found he rather liked them; they were friendly and reasonable, not like the extremists he felt he was fighting. All except one. One man was the epitome of the sort of joyless Puritan Hind hated, refusing to drink and eat with them on the grounds he had no money – though shortly before he'd been boasting that he had

£200 he was going to invest. Hind decided he was going to be made the example.

Anyone else would have burst into the man's room with a pistol at the ready. Not Hind. He went down the road to a nearby skinner's shop, where he bought a bearskin. He then returned to the inn and dressed himself up in the skin. *Then* he burst into the man's room, roaring and clawing at the air. Actually there was a certain logic in it; no one was ever going to believe the man's description of his assailant. The victim ran screaming from the room; unfortunately the inn's mastiff then came running in and went for the bear. After all, one of the things the Puritans had outlawed was bear-baiting – they weren't all bad by any means – and the dog clearly felt it was getting out of practice. Hind quickly snatched up a leg of mutton and tossed it to the mastiff to keep it quiet; then he emptied the contents of the man's bag into his own, bundled the bearskin up the chimney, and ran for it.

But Hind still tried as far as possible to practice his crimes on the Parliamentarian leaders. He managed to catch Bradshaw in a coach between Sherborne and Shaftesbury, and told him to stand and deliver. Bradshaw threatened him with the law, but Hind replied,

> *I fear you not, nor ever a king-killing son of a whore alive. If you do not give me your money instantly, I'll send you out of this world in a moment, without any benefit of clergy at all.*

In fact Bradshaw tried to cheat him but failed, and yet lived to tell the tale. Because one thing all the stories of Hind agreed on; he never killed anyone as part of his highwayman activities.

This poses an interesting question: how does a highwayman who is known for never killing his victims survive in the business? Surely the next man he holds up will simply call his bluff? Perhaps his lack of violence was more chance than policy – he must have let off a few shots in the affray with Cromwell. At any rate, his luck in that respect was about to run out. One thing his greatest apologists couldn't deny: James Hind was about to turn cold-blooded murderer.

It was near Maidenhead that Hind lay in wait for another of his arch-enemies, Colonel Harrison. The robbery went according to plan, and Hind set off with his booty. But by a freak chance everything went wrong. One of Harrison's servants, George Sympson, had been sent off after Harrison with an urgent message and arrived on the scene just after Hind had completed his robbery and was riding away. Believing that the hoofbeats he heard were Harrison coming after him to take back his property, Hind wheeled round and fired at Sympson, blowing him off his horse and killing him.

Highway robbery was always a serious crime, but somehow Hind had always contrived to make it seem a light-hearted joke. Suddenly it wasn't funny any more. The renewed hunt for him may have been one of the reasons he fled to The Hague to meet the future Charles II's council and discuss how he could help them in their attempts to restore him to the throne. From there he went to Ireland and enlisted with the Marquess of Ormonde, then via the Scilly Isles and the Isle of Man to Scotland, where he joined the Duke of Buckingham's forces. It was with them that he fought at the Battle of Worcester, the abortive attempt to put Prince Charles on the English throne, and when the Royalist troops were scattered he slowly traveled on foot to London, using the name of James Brown. Once there, he lodged at Denzy the Barber's in Fleet Street, and it was there he was arrested while lying in bed. A former colleague had recognized him and told the authorities.

Hind was taken to Newgate and locked up securely – far more securely than the average prisoner in those days. No one was taking any risk of him getting away. It wasn't just that he was a highwayman and a murderer; he was also a known Royalist who had several times done service in the King's forces. He wasn't being treated as a simple criminal, but as a traitor to the regime. Indeed on 10 November 1651 he was examined at Whitehall, where

> *divers questions were put to him in relation to his late engagement with Charles Stuart and whether he was the man that accompanied the Scots King for the furtherance of his escape. To which Hind answered that he never saw the King since the fight at Worcester, neither did he know of his getting off the field, but he now was glad to hear that he had made so happy an escape.*

One thing was certain: Hind wasn't going to deny his allegiances. It was all of a piece with his general character – there was nothing cunning or calculating about him. He lived flamboyantly, and he was prepared to die the same way. 'I owe a debt to God,' he said, 'and a debt I must pay, blessed be His Name.'

And yet it looked as if he would escape. The actual charge brought against him was for the murder of George Sympson, a capital crime which would deal with him neatly. The odd thing was that Hind was an educated man, but he failed to read the neck verse. To claim benefit of clergy and hence avoid the death penalty, an accused man had to prove he could read; this was normally done by asking him to read out the first verse of Psalm 51. Hind should have had no difficulty, and yet he failed. O M Meades has put forward a possible reason: that Hind was used to the Coverdale translation of the Book of Common Prayer, but was given the Authorized Version to read and didn't look at it closely. But still, it remains something of a mystery.

Yet ultimately it didn't matter. The day after his death sentence was pronounced, the Act of Oblivion came into force, pardoning all crimes except high treason and wiping the slate clean for all criminals going through the courts. Hind was saved. Except that they hanged him anyway.

Executing a Royalist agent for highway robbery was an excellent way of avoiding creating a martyr. Not only did it avoid openly punishing someone for loyalty to the King, it also made a clear comment on the sort of villain who supported Charles Stuart. But once that was no longer possible, the authorities gave up pretending; they charged him with high treason, the one crime which wasn't covered by the Act of Oblivion.

This was bad news for James Hind. At least as a highwayman he would only have been hanged. But as a traitor, he would be subject to hanging, drawing and quartering – cut down from the gallows while still alive and his entrails ripped out to be burned before his face, before his body was hacked into pieces and displayed around the town. Still he went to his execution as flippantly as he had lived. 'I value it not threepence to lose my life in so good a cause', he said on mounting the scaffold. Earlier he had regretted not dying on the battlefield at Worcester.

So, hero or villain? Depends on your political leanings to an extent, but George Sympson might have had something to say on the matter. Once a highwayman, always a highwayman.

CHAPTER 20

Giles Covington – The Gentle Art of Railroading
c. 1787–91

Daniel Harris was an ambitious man, and no fool. His chosen route to the top was the prison service, or what passed for a prison service back in the 1780s. He'd reached the heights of Clerk of Works in Oxford Gaol, and the next step was Gaolkeeper itself, but that post was already occupied by the delightfully named Solomon Wisdom. Wisdom had no intention of going anywhere; it was up to Harris to persuade him otherwise.

Fortunately for him, Wisdom was nowhere near as devious and clever as his opponent. For a start he was a Keeper of the old school; he'd failed to spot that the 1780s were a period of big change for prisons and houses of correction in England. The publication of Howard's *State of the Prisons in England and Wales* in 1777 had persuaded magistrates the length and breadth of England to look at problems of corruption, of crowding prisoners in one large room, of the lack of resources to feed and clothe the inmates. Wisdom was having none of it. He was repugnant, as one magistrate put it, to every scheme for reform introduced in the gaol.

With the magistrates seriously antagonistic to Wisdom, it only remained for Harris to find the

St George's tower, part of Oxford Gaol dating from the Norman Conquest and still in existence today.

The cartoon of 'Daniel Damnable' Harris, which cost Solomon Wisdom his job.

grounds for a trial of strength. He did this, ironically, over a dunghill: the night soil of the prisoners which Wisdom insisted on heaping up by the foundations of the building as had always been done, and Harris wanted moved out into the yard to avoid blocking the drainage. After a prolonged tug of war, in which the substance in question was dragged back and forth across the premises, Harris warned Wisdom that he would complain formally to the magistrates if it was found piled by the foundations again. Wisdom retaliated by sticking an insulting caricature of Harris on the prison gate – *Daniel Damnable on the Dunghill* – and delivered himself into the hands of his enemy.

Harris moved heaven and earth (and nightsoil) to pin responsibility for the drawing on Wisdom, and in so doing accidentally uncovered other abuses of the Gaolkeeper's position. The prisoner who had actually drawn the cartoon claimed that Wisdom ran the prison as a reign of terror, victimising anyone who refused to assist him in his dubious activities. Harris and the magistrates had the evidence they needed; Wisdom was dismissed and Harris took over his post.

It was reform of a sort, but only from brutal corruption to corruption of a much more subtle cast.

Which brings us to the matter of Giles Freeman Covington. Covington was a man with a talent for bad company; just how bad he was to discover when it was too late. In particular, three of his chosen associates were John Castle, Richard Kilby and Charles Evans Shury, as unpleasant a trio of villains as ever stole pheasants out of Bushey Park or made off with a haul of church plate. Covington was the baby of the pack; aged about 20 in 1787, he was described as five feet nine inches high, very stout and well made, pale complexion, light grey eyes, long visage, large, long nose, remarkably gruff in speech, walks very upright, rather swaggering in his gait. If that sounds like a wanted poster description, it's not surprising: it is.

What brought Covington to the attention of the authorities was the fate of David Chartres, a Scotch pedlar. On Monday 8 October, Chartres was trading at Abingdon Fair and making a success of it; on his way home to Toot Baldon he dropped in at a pub at Water Turnpike for refreshment, and after leaving was never seen alive again. His body was found in a ditch near Lord Harcourt's Park in Nuneham Courteney three days later, lying in a pool of blood; his head had been beaten in with a hedge stake, at least five separate wounds being visible. Needless to say, the cash he had been carrying was nowhere to be found.

The authorities started investigating the usual suspects: Robert 'Jolly Robin' Latimer, well-known shady dealer of Warborough,

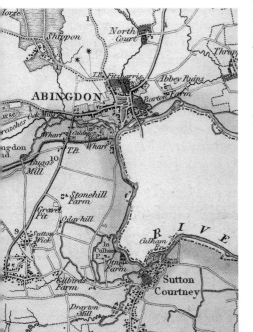

Benjamin Woolsgrove, similar of Toot Baldon, and especially James Carter of Nuneham, who was known particularly to dislike the victim. But all these faded out in the face of actual witnesses; John King and James Patey had been returning from the Fair to Dorchester when they noticed Chartres making his way through

David Chartres crossed the county boundary to reach the site of his murder – from Abingdon in Berkshire …

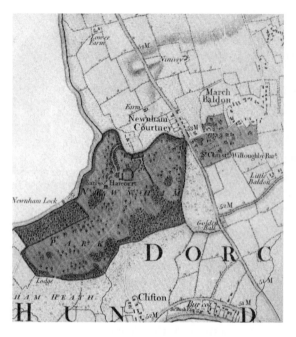

... to Nuneham Courtney in Oxfordshire.

the fields just on from Water Turnpike, and some little way behind him a gang of four men, three of whom were identifiable as Castle, Kilby and Shury. Since this was hardly illegal they had continued on their way, when suddenly they were frozen to the spot by a hideous cry coming from the direction in which Chartres and the others had been going. No one ever asked the witnesses why they failed to go and investigate; the court probably took it as read that two unarmed men would not venture too near a gang of four, three of whom at least were known thugs. The late eighteenth century was not a time for pleasant country rambles without an armed escort.

Still, they were tempted to face the four men, or at least three of them, in court for the sake of the reward. On the discovery of Chartres' body, the Justice of the Peace Christopher Willoughby had put up a reward of ten guineas for information leading to the apprehension of the murderers, which sounds quite generous until one learns he was offering exactly the same to find out what reprobate stole his laundry off the washing line a few weeks earlier. However, Lord Harcourt, who felt personally affronted by people slaughtering one another on his land, raised the stakes to seventy guineas, which was temptation indeed. Unfortunately, King and Patey were unable to identify the fourth man; it was left to the villains themselves to do that.

Once the trio were in custody, a surprising number of witnesses crawled out of the woodwork to provide damning evidence which they had unaccountably forgotten about up to that point. In particular Peter Peckman of the Half Moon in Abingdon came up with some hearsay which was of no little interest to the magistrates. According to him, Joseph Crawford, a bargeman, came into the pub one morning and recounted a conversation he'd had with Castle, in which Castle claimed he was

> *one of the persons who swung the woman over Culham Bridge* [an earlier unsolved murder] *and that he had held either of the hands or the legs and that he helped throw her over the bridge, and that he knew who did the Scotchman, that he was present, and that after they said he was dead a woman who was likewise preset said, 'Damn his blood, draw him among the stinging nettles'.*

Bargemen were not the most highly esteemed members of society, but as a result tended to pick up interesting information on their travels; another, John Brown, claimed 'he has heard John Castle say that if he was taken and admitted in evidence, that he would discover who the persons were that committed the murder at Culham Bridge and the man at Nuneham'.

The rolling parkland of Nuneham Estate, scene of the grisly murder of David Chartres.

Castle's big mouth had dropped him in it beyond hope of recourse; Evans and Shury began to wonder if they could use this fact to wriggle off the hook themselves. Covington was another associate of theirs, and being out of custody was in no position to deny any accusations made against him. He probably was the unidentified fourth man, but whether he committed the murder is another matter entirely. Locked away in Oxford Gaol awaiting trial, Shury suggested to Kilby that he should tell the authorities all he knew. This didn't strike Kilby as a particularly bright idea: 'Then I shall injure you, Charles – but I suppose you want me to confess that you may do me.' 'No, boy,' grinned Shury, 'for you shall be evidence along with me.' If the pair of them turned King's Evidence against Castle and Covington, there was a chance they might walk out of the court free men.

Kilby followed Shury's plan, with just one tiny alteration; he threw Shury to the wolves along with Castle and Covington. No point in taking risks, and Shury left alive would always have a hold over him. Besides, the court might not stand for two men slipping out of its clutches, but one might have a chance. 'In the afternoon of the day on which the murder was committed,' he said,

Shury applied to him and two other accomplices, informing them that he would help them to a good booty in robbing an old Scotchman on his way home. That they afterwards met at Shury's house, where they agreed to the proposal, and about five o'clock in the evening Shury and Castle went first, and in about ten minutes were followed by him and Covington. That they joined company near the Water Turnpike, but about Ditch End again separated, Kilby keeping the path whilst Shury, Covington and Castle kept to the left towards the river. That they all four again joined company, and as soon as Chartres had got over the stile, Shury struck him a violent blow on the head with the hedge stake, which blow was immediately followed by others from him and Covington till they judged him dead, himself and Castle being all this while a few yards distant, till Covington called for assistance to roll the body into the ditch. That Castle and Kilby returned together to Abingdon to Shury's house, and met with

him and Covington, where the booty was divided, Shury giving
each of them in gold and silver ten guineas, saying, 'Now, my
boys, let us be true to each other.'

Despite the best attempts of Shury's counsel to discredit him,
Kilby waved his two friends off to the gallows, while he walked
out of court a free man. The pardon for which he had paid by
stabbing the rest of the gang in the back cost the authorities
£88/10/6d in hard cash, so they wanted to make the most of
it. Covington had been fingered, so Covington was going to
swing no matter how long it took.

And it took a while. While all this was going on, Covington
had married, had a son, and joined the navy, showing no great
urgency in any of these things. It was 1791 before he returned
to England and stepped once again on British soil, where to
his great surprise he was immediately arrested and whisked off
to Oxford to stand trial. On his arrival, *Jackson's Oxford
Journal* referred to him as 'this most atrocious offender' – no
namby-pamby nonsense about a man being innocent until
proved guilty – and this was just the beginning of what was not
so much an investigation into the guilt of a suspect as a
determination that something which looked like justice was
going to be seen to be done.

The problem was that Covington wouldn't play along with
the deal. He most unreasonably persisted in claiming that he
was innocent, and when it came down to it, the only actual
evidence against him was Kilby's. King and Patey had never
been able to identify the fourth man they saw by the Water
Turnpike, and Kilby was already in it up to his neck; he was
just as likely to have done it as anyone else. All of which
bothered the authorities not one iota; they'd got Covington,
and no one was going to deprive them of him.

In court, 'Kilby sayeth on his oath that Giles Covington
struck David Chartres after he was knocked down by Charles
Evans Shury, and that this deponent, Shury and John Castle
were all present when the said Chartres was murdered'. At
that point in the trial proceedings, Covington broke out of the
prisoner's box and went for Kilby. He got as far as raising his
fist for a blow before the court officials subdued him and

dragged him back. Still protesting his innocence, Covington was dragged back to the cells, while the court hurriedly found him guilty and sentenced him to hang. But this wasn't the way it was supposed to go. Covington's outburst had made a lot of people wonder whether just possibly Kilby was the one lying, and the last thing the magistrates wanted was the suspicion of a miscarriage of justice hanging over their heads. It was at this point that one or two odd things began to happen.

The first thing was the appearance of the mysterious Mr Lovegrove of Wallingford. Mr Lovegrove was a gentleman without an address, who failed to date his letters, but he may well have existed; there were Lovegroves in Wallingford. There was also a Joseph Deadman in Brightwell. It was what these two claimed that was odd. Lovegrove wrote a letter to Christopher Willoughby, the magistrate:

Sir – There is a shopkeeper of respectable character named Joseph Deadman of Brightwell, Berks, near this place, who was some time since in Oxford Castle, and on observing to Giles Covington (with whom he had once been in company at Sutton) that he was sorry to see him in that situation, his answer was so remarkable that out of love to public justice I thought it necessary to send it to you. I shall follow the rest of them and die with a lie in my mouth as they did. Whether you shall or shall not see it necessary to subpoena Deadman, you will be so obliging as not to mention I have given you this information.

Remarkable indeed. Covington, who has steadfastly protested his innocence from the beginning, tells the truth to a man he knows only casually, who mysteriously happens to be passing through Oxford Castle, not a place on most people's daily route. A respectable shopkeeper who nevertheless knows this villain well enough to be trusted with a terrible secret. Which somehow Lovegrove finds out about, but insists that his name shall not be mentioned. The whole thing feels very odd, and extremely convenient from the authorities' point of view.

Covington was hanged on 7 March 1791. The previous evening he dictated a letter from the condemned cell to Willoughby, still claiming he was innocent:

The letter Giles Covington wrote from the condemned cell the night before his execution.

There is no doubt that the poor man lost his life, but, Sir Willoughby, it [is] not found out [who did] it, and so you will find when tis too late for me. I hope you and your family will live to find Giles Freeman Covington died innocent, and then I hope you will relieve the widow that is left behind, if bedlam is not to be her doom.

From the gallows he flung down another letter insisting he was innocent, which mysteriously vanished instantly, and with the parting words 'Beware of Kilby!' he fell through the trap. But just because he was dead didn't mean the authorities were rid of him.

More and more people were having doubts about the case. The continued protestations of innocence, the lack of any firm evidence, the way that Kilby had clearly bought his own life at the expense of the other three, were not making the magistrates look good. Fortunately for them, they now had the devious Daniel Harris on the payroll.

Harris wrote to Willoughby on the day of the execution:

Covington persisted in his innocence to the last with respect to the murder…. I think some well directed paragraph should appear in the newspapers, to entirely clear up the business. The circumstance of all three persisting in their innocence at the last moment causes some to have their doubts, I apprehend.

And so it was that *Jackson's Oxford Journal*, which prefaced the trial by calling Covington 'this most atrocious offender', concluded its reporting with a masterpiece of non-sequitur and woolly argument:

> *Having mounted the drop, he threw over a paper which he desired might be read aloud; it denied, as his confederates had also done, the fact for which he suffered. He had also confessed, among other things, to sacrilegiously robbing St Nicholas Church, Abingdon, in company with Shury; and, in an unguarded moment, with bitter imprecations, charged Kilby with falsehood and perjury in giving testimony that any of the blows were given by him to Chartres. After conviction he acknowledged divers crimes which at present it would be imprudent to divulge, but which would remove any doubt, could any remain, of his guilt. Hence we have only to lament the wickedness and depravity of human nature, that any hardened wretches should thus dare, in their dying moments, by attempting to impose upon credulous minds, insult an already offended deity.*

Which, reduced to its component parts, reads: there is other evidence that Covington is guilty but we're not telling you what it is, a man who robs a church would of course commit murder, and anyone who thinks that our reasoning is a little faulty here is a credulous fool. Harris' struggles with Solomon Wisdom had given him a good grounding in propaganda.

But even Harris couldn't cover all the bases. As supergrasses go, Kilby proved to be an absolute pain. Having escaped the gallows, you might think he'd be happy to sneak off into obscurity, but Kilby was greedy and wouldn't let go. He'd been tried and acquitted for the murder, which left him in a strong position. In a very short time he was putting the bite on Harris, who was turning in desperation to Willoughby for guidance:

> *Kilby has wrote to me to say that he has got work at Cotton End near Northampton, that he at present lodges in a public house, and wishes me to send him some money, that may help him buy goods to go into a private house. I can't help thinking his application somewhat too early....*

This was no witness relocation scheme; Kilby had turned King's Evidence and been rewarded with his freedom. What made him think that he had the right to be supported in his future life by the authorities? And why, apart from the matter of timing, are the authorities going along with it? The precise nature of the deal which seems to have been brokered by Harris begins to look very odd indeed.

Covington's skeleton is in the public domain to this day; after his execution his body was delivered to the anatomy school, who used him as a teaching aid for many years before putting him into a storeroom. When he was rediscovered, he became an exhibit in the Museum of Oxford. On the two-hundredth anniversary of his execution an attempt was made to get him a retrospective pardon, but the Home Office declined on the grounds that no fresh evidence had come to light.

Today, the evidence which hanged him wouldn't have got him six months.

The sworn testimony of Kilby which sent his friends to the gallows.

CHAPTER 21

James Millin – A Curious Thing to Shoot a Man through a Hedge 1824

The Forest of Wychwood was a standing temptation to poor labouring men. The haunt of a vast array of game, it lured those whose business or trade was going badly to become poachers, helping themselves to the stocks available. Such were William James and Henry Pittaway, but their change of career ended in tragedy.

James was born in Burford, the only surviving son of a labourer, in 1776. He wasn't an uneducated man; in fact he'd been at the Free School there for seven years before being apprenticed to a slater and plasterer. After completing his apprenticeship he married his cousin Mary and moved to Taynton, where the couple had their fair share of domestic tragedy; of their six children, both the first and last were born both mentally and physically disabled. What effect this had on James is impossible to say, but he started neglecting his business and took to deer stealing. Pittaway was a labourer in Swinbrook, only half James' age, but similarly inclined to ignore his proclaimed calling and go hunting for deer.

Unfortunately for them, the game in Wychwood Forest belonged to Lord Churchill, who had a very efficient gamekeeper, James Millin. Millin soon had his eye on James,

Wychwood Forest as it still looked when Millin was gamekeeper.

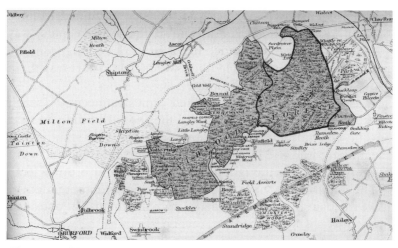

The extent of Wychwood Forest in the early nineteenth century, before deforestation, is shown in dark shading.

and before long had him charged with stealing venison. James was furious, and informed anyone who cared to listen that he would as soon shoot Millin's head off as he would the head of a butterfly. 'Revenge is sweet', he growled. 'Let the Lord pay it.'

He evidently announced that he could easily sneak up on the ever-vigilant Millin, by coming up on him behind a hedge. 'It is a curious thing to shoot a man through a hedge', remarked a certain Mr Prattley who was listening to him. 'It is a curious thing', replied James. 'But if a man cannot rest till he has done it, what is he to do? And if ever he is taken to, he is sure to be hanged for it.'

Pittaway too had declared a certain animosity towards Millin, saying he wouldn't mind killing him if there were no witnesses around – apparently feeling that witnesses to the intention didn't count – and that there would be murder done in the Forest that summer. What's more, Pittaway had a gun, which he unfortunately kept in the bedroom he shared with his young niece. At six o'clock on 15 June 1824 the girl saw the gun in its usual place. When she went up to bed at seven-thirty she noticed the gun was missing. She thought no more of this, until the subsequent events of that evening emerged.

At about eight that evening, Millin passed by James' house on his rounds. Pittaway was following him, slipped into James' house, and the two men emerged and followed the keeper towards Hensgrove coppice. At quarter to nine, Millin's brother Joseph, who was also one of the local keepers, was startled to hear what sounded like a gunshot coming from the direction of the coppice. He ran towards it, and part way there came across James and Pittaway.

'Was that you who fired?' asked James innocently. Joseph said he hadn't, but that he'd heard the shot. 'But did you hear anyone cry murder?' James continued. 'We were standing by the milking stile and heard a shot fired in Hensgrove and a cry of murder, and we thought it was the cry of your brother Jem.'

The taunt must have been obvious; Joseph pretended to leave the pair, but instead hid and watched them. They strolled over to where Millin lay just beyond a gap in the wall round the coppice, and Joseph quickly made his way round to see his brother. James and Pittaway came up to offer assistance in carrying the corpse home, and that was when they got their big shock. It wasn't a corpse.

Millin's thigh was broken and he was losing blood fast; he was in a bad way. But not so bad that he couldn't tell his brother what had happened, and the appearance of James and Pittaway on the scene simply added weight to his story. Within half an hour of being carried back to his home he died, but by then he'd given all the information needed for the prosecution of the two poachers. With the assistance of Pittaway's niece, who obligingly gave evidence on the absence of her uncle's gun during the crucial time, the jury had no hesitation. They retired for only fifteen minutes, before returning a verdict of guilty on both men.

William James proved to be accurate in his predictions; he was taken and he was hanged with his associate. Both men went to the gallows protesting their innocence, but effectively they'd stitched themselves up even without the evidence of the keeper, by announcing their intentions in advance. Which would almost be an argument for them not being guilty, were it not for the depressing regularity with which minor villains of the time went out of their way to lay a trail to their own doors.

William James and Henry Pittaway pay the price for their crimes.

CHAPTER 22

Burned at the Stake – Cranmer, Latimer and Ridley
1554–55

Of all the foul deeds one human being can commit on another, burning someone to death in the town ditch must be a candidate for the worst. And yet it was not that uncommon. All over England witches were tried and executed in the flames. And for heretics it was a regular means of dispatch. Since what constituted heresy changed with successive monarchs, some agility was needed to keep away from the pyre. For the ordinary individual there was no problem, but senior churchmen could have difficulties.

One of the most dangerous times in history was the brief reign of Mary Tudor, which earned her the nickname 'Bloody Mary'. While Protestant apologists have perhaps made the period sound worse than it was, it was bad enough. It was particularly unpleasant for Bishops Latimer and Ridley and Archbishop Thomas Cranmer, who found themselves at the receiving end of Mary's cure for allergy to the Pope.

Cranmer had already been tried for High Treason and condemned to be hanged, drawn and quartered, but Mary saw

Ralph Agas' map of Oxford in 1585, showing Bocardo, St Mary's Church, and just to the left of the 's' in St Michael's, the spot where the martyrs were burned.

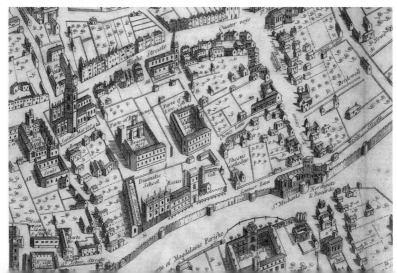

Bocardo, where the three clerics were kept prisoner during their trials.

this as a fallback position; what mattered about Cranmer was his status as a figurehead for those hostile to the Catholic Church, and it was on this ground that she wanted to meet and defeat him. In March 1554, the three clerics were taken to Oxford to be tried, and imprisoned in Bocardo for the duration. Bocardo was a lockup often used to house debtors; it was situated over the top of the north gate to the City, spanning Cornmarket by the church of St Michael at the Northgate (which houses a door said to be that of the clerics' cell). Occasionally they were allowed to stretch their legs along that part of the City walls. Today it seems odd to think that they would be strolling through the upper floor of Boswell's department store.

And just outside the City walls, along the line of what is now Broad Street, lay the town ditch, the equivalent of a moat to lend height to the ramparts. No one in their right mind would try to burn so much as a side of pork within the walls; the timber buildings would take light immediately. In fact during the Civil War a century later one soldier did try to roast a stolen pig within the walls and succeeded in burning down about a quarter of the old town. If the three bishops were to be executed, it would be outside the walls where everyone else would be safe.

The church of St Mary the Virgin, where the trials took place.

The point of bringing the prisoners to Oxford was that it was a centre of academic debate; simply telling the Protestant leaders that they were wrong and condemning them wouldn't go far towards convincing their followers not to continue with their heretical beliefs in private. They had to be proved to be in error in public debate. Imprisoning them in the same cell was probably a bad move in this regard, as they were able to hone their debating skills on one another and plug any holes in one another's arguments. The location had the additional advantage that there were plenty of supporters of their evangelical cause in London, and Mary could do without violent public demonstrations of support.

On 14 April the three were taken to the University Church of St Mary the Virgin, given the subjects to be debated (transubstantiation and the mass), and told to put their views forward separately without collusion. The result was not a great triumph for their Catholic opponents. Cranmer, refusing the chance to sit down, made it look as if his opponents didn't understand the theological terms they were using; Ridley was a ruthless debater and the judges had to beg him to shorten his extensive written text; Latimer, who was actually old and ill, played the simple old man card and didn't give his opponents any opening to force him into a formal statement of belief. When Cranmer's session was transferred to the Divinity School (now part of the Bodleian Library) the proceedings were so chaotic that Weston, the moderator of the proceedings, accidentally described his own Catholic views as heresy and was practically laughed out of the building.

Despite this, at the end of the week Weston announced that the bishops had been beaten in argument by their Catholic opponents. Says who, the bishops retorted in rather more formal language. But of course there had never been any chance they would be allowed to win – this was part of the systematic return of England to Catholicism, and accepting that Cranmer and his friends had any truth on their side would have destroyed everything. However, things now went rather into abeyance, and the three found themselves removed from Bocardo for a while and lodged with the Mayor and bailiffs of the town. The point was that Mary was determined to do everything by the book. England was still not formally reconciled to papal obedience, and wouldn't be until November 1554. Only then did the English bishops technically have the power to enquire into heresy.

The burnings of heretics began in London in early 1555, and it was obvious that the authorities were working up to Cranmer, Latimer and Ridley – the bishops themselves believed that it was expected that the second-rank Protestant leaders would break easily once isolated from the three. In fact Cranmer's trial didn't begin until 12 September 1555 in the University Church, and even then no one in England was given the right to judge him – that privilege was reserved for the Pope himself. There were some shaky moments, but Cranmer maintained his stance throughout; indeed in a submission to Queen Mary afterwards he said that if anyone could convince him that the Pope was right he would submit 'not only to kiss his feet, but another part also'. That sort of dubious joke did nothing to endear him to his enemies.

Ridley and Latimer, less important than the Archbishop, were tried later in the month and, since the Pope was not taking a personal interest, found guilty. On 16 October they were led out to execution past Bocardo so that Cranmer could get a good look. As an odd sidelight, this meant that they turned the corner by the church of St Mary Magdalen; exactly four hundred years later, when England had been Protestant for so long that its Catholic past was all but forgotten by all except historians and theologians, St Mary Magdalen was described under its vicar Colin Stephenson as being 'the highest Anglo-Catholic church in England'. Cranmer was taken out onto the roof to watch his friends burn, in the hope that it would terrify him into backing down.

It was at the stake that Latimer made his most famous observation to his companion: 'Be of good comfort, Master Ridley, and play the man. We shall this day light such a candle, by God's grace, in England, as I trust shall never be put out.' This was all very well for him. He died quickly of smoke inhalation. By contrast, Ridley's brother-in-law, George Shipside, tried to speed Ridley's death by piling on more fuel, and only succeeded in blocking the flames and making Ridley's torment last longer.

As might be expected, watching all of this did not put Cranmer in a cheerful state of mind. While watching the burning, he was observed to fall to his knees, tear his cap off his head, and forcibly

The burning of Thomas Cranmer, from Fox's Book of Martyrs.

express his horror. This was clearly a good time for his opponents to work on him and try to make him recant his beliefs. He was moved to Christ Church, and his resolve began to crumble. While he was there he had been formally condemned in Rome and the decision was slowly returning by messenger to England. On 24 February the writ was issued for his burning; the date was set for 7 March and Cranmer, by now back in Bocardo after annoying a number of Catholic divines with his careful arguments, suddenly realized that time had run out. He signed his first recantation of his beliefs. The Catholics were delighted – so much so that they made a fatal mistake.

They rushed the recantation into print, not noticing that it still bore the signatures of the two Spanish friars, de Soto and Villagarcia, who had been instrumental in wringing it out of him. The Privy Council immediately put out a writ for the return of all the copies, but too late to stop some leaking onto the open market. The point was not so much that the signatures made it obvious that Cranmer had been 'assisted' to recant – no one imagined it would be otherwise – as that the Spanish were absolutely detested in England at that time, a fact not unconnected with the Queen marrying Philip of Spain. Anything with a Spanish name attached to it was instantly ridiculed. The recantation was worse than useless.

Meanwhile another spoke had just been stuck in the Catholics' wheel. A huge comet had appeared over southern England; this was heralded as foretelling the Last Judgement, and executing the Archbishop of Canterbury (which Cranmer still was, for all the crimes he was accused of) would seem to fit in quite well with the idea. Crowds gathered at the Bocardo, threatening to storm it and set Cranmer free. Terrified of major revolt, Mary put off the execution. Still, it gave her clergy the chance to wring another recantation out of Cranmer; they were a bit more cautious with this one.

It might be thought that now Cranmer was supposedly a good Catholic again, there was no need to burn him; but that wasn't the way the sixteenth-century mind worked. A new date of 21 March was set for the execution. Cranmer would be taken to the University Church where he would publicly confess his errors and announce that he had returned to the true faith, then he would be dragged off to follow Latimer and Ridley. At last the authorities could breathe a sigh of relief. Of course they weren't in Bocardo on the evening of 20 March, when Cranmer gave a coin to a servant girl to pray for him, saying he thought the prayers of a good layperson better than those of a bad priest. If they had been, they might have got an inkling of the nightmare waiting for them the next day. The action was not exactly in line with Catholic theology.

Cranmer stood up in St Mary's on the morning of 21 March and started to go through the prayers and penitence which had been agreed in advance with the authorities. True, he missed out the Angelus to Our Lady, but that was probably an oversight, they told themselves. In fact they were quite relaxed about the whole thing when it suddenly went wrong.

The assembled Catholic clergy suddenly came to their senses to hear Cranmer denouncing them from the pulpit. All his recantation, he declared, 'was contrary to the truth which I thought it my heart, and written for fear of death'. Before they could reach him, he'd firmly announced that he was a staunch Protestant, despised the Catholics, and had only ever said otherwise because they were threatening to burn him. Now that they were going to burn him anyway, there was no point in pretending any more. 'As for the Pope, I refuse him as Christ's enemy and Antichrist!' he yelled, a split second before he was forcibly dragged from the pulpit. In just over one minute, he had done more damage than the Catholics would have thought possible.

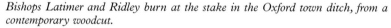

Bishops Latimer and Ridley burn at the stake in the Oxford town ditch, from a contemporary woodcut.

The church erupted in an uproar. Fighting broke out. The authorities grabbed the Archbishop and hustled him off to the stake outside the walls; no solemn procession – they had to get rid of this man as fast as possible. Villagarcia, the Spanish friar, looked shellshocked. He turned on Cranmer and snarled, you'd have stuck to your recantation if we'd offered to let you live! Cranmer looked at him with contempt. Of course I would, he replied. We're all afraid of a painful death.

They burned Cranmer without delay. It was well attested that he stuck his right hand into the flames, saying that the hand had

The memorial set up to the Oxford Martyrs by St Mary Magdalen church in 1841–3.

offended by signing his recantation so it should burn first. Less plausible was the story that after the burning his heart was found untouched in the ashes; but whatever the Catholics did, they couldn't scotch the tale. Eventually they decided to admit it had happened but to claim that it was due to heart disease. Not very convincing.

There was an ironic tailpiece to the story. Throughout the whole saga two of the Oxford bailiffs had been saddled with many of the charges of looking after the three clerics. When the whole thing went sour, Mary neglected to reimburse them – they were paid only £20 out of the £63 they were owed. Eventually they gave up trying to get the money out of her and waited until her death, when the Protestant Queen Elizabeth ascended to the throne. Then they petitioned Archbishop Parker. Parker found himself organizing a whip-round among the clergy who had been Cranmer's friends and disciples to pay for the means of having him executed. And astonishingly he managed to raise the money.

'The case is miserable, but the debt is just', said one of his colleagues. No reason why the bailiffs should suffer. All the same, it must have stuck in their throats.

CHAPTER 23

Child Murder –
The Worst Crime of All?
1858

Different crimes for different ages. We tend to reserve our greatest horror for crimes against those whom we see as being particularly defenceless, and in twenty-first century society crimes against children come high up the list. It can come as a shock to our modern sensibilities, therefore, to find out how common such crimes could be in previous centuries, and how leniently they could be treated.

This was nothing to do with the often-stated view that parents of the mediaeval and early modern period refused to grow too closely attached to children who were at the mercy of a high mortality rate. Based largely on circumstantial evidence, such as successive children being baptized with the same name, the view fails to stand up to the evidence of diaries, letters and wills, which show as close a concern about the welfare of individual children as anything in the past century. Rather it was connected with such matters as poor relief and the position of women in society, combining to create a situation in which the life of a new-born infant could be seen as a lesser sacrifice.

Mary Merrick was the twenty-two-year-old daughter of John Merrick, a farm labourer who worked for a Mr Paine at Haddenham in Buckinghamshire. When Paine decided to take another farm at Finmere in

Map of Finmere, where Mary Merrick disposed of her dead baby.

Oxfordshire, John Merrick followed him to work there, leaving his cottage in Haddenham in the charge of Mary.

On 30 January 1858 Mary came on a visit to see her father and her brother Mark, who lodged at the house of a railway policeman by the name of John Watson. His room was large enough for two, and it was decided that Mary should share it with him while she was in Finmere. She had intended to make a flying visit, but the weather was so bad that she was unable to return to Haddenham, and was still staying with her brother on Thursday 4 February when it became obvious that she was not well. Hannah Watson, the railway policeman's wife, was concerned, but Mary told her that her illness was not unexpected and arose from natural causes; she went to bed early at eight o'clock, and subsequently Hannah brought her up a little elder wine.

Shortly afterwards Mary was heard moaning, but no one thought this was anything unusual as she had assured Hannah that she had always suffered badly on similar occasions. Her brother Mark went up to bed in the same room a couple of hours later, but did not hear her make any noise either then or during the night. On the following morning he got up early, leaving her in bed; she rose at about half past seven, came downstairs, and ate her breakfast. She seemed to be in much better spirits, and after breakfast went back upstairs to put on her bonnet and shawl to return home.

When she came back down, she had a bundle on her arm which, she told Hannah, contained some things her brother had given her out of his box. She left the house at eight o'clock, saying she would call at Mr Paine's farmhouse on her way to see her father. Indeed she was seen with her bundle at about quarter past eight by George Freeman, a local labourer.

At about nine that same morning, one George Tomkins was walking down the road which led from the Watsons' cottage to Paine's farmhouse when he noticed a piece of canvas stained with blood hanging from one of the rails bordering the track. On closer investigation he discovered the naked body of a new-born child lying in the ditch beyond the rails. It seemed that the child had been wrapped in the canvas, which someone had attempted to fling over the rails into the ditch but which had snagged as it went past. Tomkins told Freeman what he had found, and Freeman recalled seeing Mary Merrick with her mysterious bundle.

Meanwhile Mary had seen her father who gave her money and food to see her home. He was already suspicious that something was going on, as he could hardly fail to notice her size and shape, and he told her he was afraid she had got herself into trouble and was in the family way. She stoutly denied this, at which he replied that in that case she must have her mother's trouble of dropsy and ought to take care of herself before it carried her off. After she'd left, Merrick heard about the discovery of the body and put two and two together. He followed his daughter to Haddenham, but arrived after nightfall and decided not to wake her; instead he stayed with a neighbour and came to find her the next morning.

Mary immediately broke down and admitted the child was hers; she said she'd been confined at the roadside on the Friday morning after leaving her lodgings, and when the child was born dead she'd panicked and thrown it into the ditch. However, this did not account for the bundle, and a local surgeon who examined the child believed it was born alive – the lungs somewhat collapsed but not sufficiently to suggest stillbirth. It seemed obvious that the child was born the previous evening between Mary retiring to bed and her brother coming upstairs two hours later; that she had hidden it until he left the following morning then taken it out in the bundle to dispose of it.

Yet the authorities declined to proceed on a murder charge. The evidence was weak, they said, and

> *the prisoner was apprehended in another county and at a considerable distance from the parish where the offence was committed, and was in such a weak state as to be unable to be removed to prison for several days after being taken into custody. And the expense of taking the witnesses to Oxford after the prisoner was received at the prison would have been very great....*

All very well; perhaps it would have been difficult to get a conviction on a charge of murder. But the same could hardly be said in the case of Eliza Nichols.

Wilkins' bird's-eye view of Deddington, sketched in 1875.

Eliza was twenty-five, and had for several years held a number of servant posts in the area. Her most recent position was at the house of Mr Fessey in Northamptonshire, and it was there, during the second week in December 1865, that she was discovered to be pregnant, and dismissed. Having no other option she returned to her mother's house at Hempton near Deddington, where her condition was already known. On Friday, 15 December she went into labour and was delivered of a healthy female child the following morning in the presence of the midwife, Mrs Shirley; various other neighbours saw the child over the next twenty-four hours and could testify there seemed to be nothing wrong with it.

On the Sunday afternoon, Eliza's sister Louisa dressed the baby and changed its nappy; Eliza then asked for another clean nappy, explaining that she wanted it for herself. This seemed a little odd to her sister, but she provided one and left the room at about quarter to four. That was the last time the child was seen alive.

At approaching six, Eliza called her sister upstairs and told her the baby had died. Louisa took the child's hand, found it was warm, and said, 'Eliza, it's not dead!' On the contrary, the mother insisted, it was extremely dead and someone must be called in to see. Louisa went to find Mrs Shirley and a neighbour, Mrs Bray, who were prevailed upon with some difficulty to come. They saw that the child was lifeless; what they also saw was a dark bruise on its neck.

At first Eliza denied being in any way responsible for her daughter's death, but on the Monday morning, when Louisa pointed out that Mr Turner, the surgeon, was coming and would certainly find out how the child died, she said, 'I will speak the truth, for God knows what I've done. I caught hold of the napkin, twisted it, and placed it round the child's throat, and put it down in the bed.' Asked if the baby had not made a noise, she said, 'A little. I thought there would not have been such a fuss about it, or I should not have done it.'

When Turner arrived she repeated her confession, and he confirmed that death was by strangulation. When her sister asked why she had done it, Eliza said she imagined the baby would just have been buried quietly and no one would have known. Mrs Bray, who was visiting, said, 'Oh dear, Eliza, how could you do this? Could you not love the child?' Crying, Eliza replied, 'Yes, I loved it a little on Saturday morning.'

It was an open-and-shut case, yet the prosecution brief went out of its way to pick holes in its own case. First it pointed out that no one was able to trace the nappy; Eliza had not left the room, and neither her mother nor her sister remembered removing it, but a search failed to find it. Then it threw doubt on the witnesses:

> *The material evidence of the prisoner's sister Louisa may be looked upon with some distrustfulness by the Court from the over eager willingness with which she gives the most condemnatory statements of her sister's guilt. It is to be feared she bears an immoral character, and is herself but the testimony of the miserable degradation in which this wretched family have been brought up.*

Mrs Shirley and Mrs Bray were next in the firing line:

> *There is a timid reluctance to give evidence on the part of Mrs Shirley, from the apparent apprehension that the exposure of her position as nurse to the bastard child is not very honorable. The other witness, Mrs Bray, gives an honest statement but is easily confused.*

The prosecution then went on to point out that a couple of years ago Eliza had suffered from two paralytic strokes, one of which temporarily robbed her of speech, while the other left her unconscious for a week, but with evident reluctance admitted that there was no proof they were affecting her mental competence. At the trial the judge picked up on this, and Turner was forced to admit that paralysis often came from a disease of the brain; if such a disease recurred, it would not necessarily be accompanied by a similar paralysis again. His evidence of the child's death was the most difficult to shake, but the defence showed that he had never before performed a post-mortem on a victim of strangulation and that all his knowledge on the matter had been gained from reading.

The defence went on to stress that confessions on the spot were the most dangerous to rely on, 'the words being often misrepresented through ignorance, malice or inattention, and being extremely liable to misconstruction, while the tone and manner in which they were made could not be known to the Jury'. The judge picked up where counsel for the defence left off, telling the jury that certain witnesses seemed to have very unreliable memories, which was important in a case where every word counted, and that Eliza's original confession seemed to have been obtained almost by threats from her sister. The jury might also think that the confession had biased Turner in his examination, so even the medical evidence was suspect. After all, on the Saturday Eliza had shown herself to be a kind, attentive mother. In fact he came as close as possible to instructing the jury to bring in a verdict, not of wilful murder but, of manslaughter.

And, after retiring for half an hour, that was what the jury did, 'strongly recommending her to mercy on account of her weak state of body and mind'. She was sentenced to twelve months imprisonment with hard labour.

Why was the entire legal system so determined to avoid harsh punishment for women murdering their new-born children? The clue can be found in the final summing up of the brief for the prosecution:

Unwilling to confront her shame and unable to face the black future of her 'Aide of Woes' she must, in that interval of an hour and a half when she was left to herself, have yielded to the sudden impulse of destroying her illegitimate offspring in the vain hope of hushed secrecy and undetected guilt.

For a poor woman, an illegitimate child closed down her entire future. Eliza had been instantly dismissed from her post of servant when her pregnancy was discovered, and since that was the only kind of job she was likely to get her forthcoming employment prospects were bleak. Carrying an illegitimate child around with her would have closed every door in her face. It was difficult enough for a single woman to survive at the best of times, and the mother of a bastard child was going to remain single.

Her only option would be to go 'on the parish'; to seek poor relief from the authorities. Their attitude could be seen in Eliza's case when her mother sought relief from the Poor Law Union for her confinement and was coldly refused. Every new pauper put the rates up, and since this worked on a local rather than a national basis every parish or Union was keen to reduce the numbers as far as possible. An individual pauper was bad enough; a mother with an illegitimate child which would need to be supported for years was their worst nightmare. Mary and Eliza could both expect the lowest level of subsistence for the rest of their lives.

Small wonder that the temptation to solve the problem at source occurred to them, and that so many women succumbed to it. Public opinion is sometimes at odds with the law, as the law is stable while opinion develops. In many eyes, these women were almost as defenceless as the children they killed, their crimes motivated not by malice but by desperation. As long as the punishment for infanticide was hanging or transportation, and as long as infanticide was the only way out of the trap, the courts would be reluctant to bring in a verdict of guilty where there was the smallest loophole through which to escape. If life was cheap in the nineteenth century, it was the law which made it so.

CHAPTER 24

Death of a Prostitute – The Dark Side of Town and Gown
1827

Oxford: city of dreaming spires and home of lost causes. Gilded youth punting down the river, only pausing to text one another on their mobile phones. But there is a darker side to the University.

For centuries, the University maintained a Jekyll and Hyde attitude to the outside world. True, there were men for whom scholarship was the goal, and whose time at Oxford was spent pursuing it. But at the same time there were many for whom the University was a form of finishing school; a place to meet other young men of their own background, to indulge in drinking bouts and behaviour of the kind now associated with certain types of football supporter. The gang of over-muscled and less than intelligent louts breaking up the local alehouse were likely to be the heirs to three or four of the most illustrious titles in England, and to a certain extent they might be indulged.

In the midst of this situation, the Proctors tried to maintain order. The office of Proctor went back to the thirteenth century as executive officer of the University, responsible for good order both in studies and conduct. Both University members and townsmen were subject to the Proctors'

Student life in the 1820s was distinctly lively.

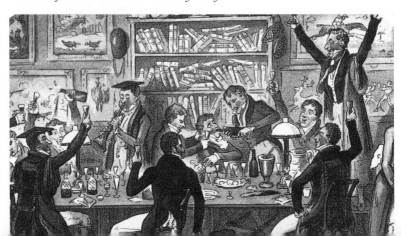

discipline, and with the assistance of the famous Bulldogs – the University Police – these officers had the right to impose fines and, in the case of students, to have an offender sent down from his college.

In the all-male society of the pre-twentieth-century University, one of the greatest problems was preventing the undergraduates seeking female companionship. Oxford was the perfect hunting ground for prostitutes, and a famous drawing by Rowlandson, *Varsity Trick – Smuggling In*, of 1810, shows a group of students sneaking a young lady into college while the Proctor watches from round a corner. The Proctors kept a register of prostitutes, whom they could expel from the city, together with a register of homicides. Had they exercised the former on Ann Crotchley, it might have prevented her joining the latter.

Ann had a slightly shady background to begin with. Aged 24 in 1827, she came from Hereford and was originally called Ann Priest; only in Oxford was she known as Crotchley. Late at night on Thursday, 6 December she was walking through the town with one Harriet Mitchell, whom she had known for no more than two days. Perhaps she thought there was safety in numbers, though the chances of the pair meeting any students were remote; college gates were closed at nine, and anyone returning later than that hour was fined. If the pair were going to do any soliciting they'd have to do it through a window. And so they did; at 11.30pm they went up to the window of a student's room in Brasenose, where some sort of gathering was in full swing, and asked for a glass of wine.

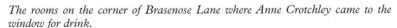

The rooms on the corner of Brasenose Lane where Anne Crotchley came to the window for drink.

The room must have looked out onto Brasenose Lane, the narrow thoroughfare linking Turl Street with Radcliffe Square. Seven or eight young men crowded to the window, and in the midst of the exchanges one of them, Houstonne John Radcliffe, told Ann that he had no wine but he could give her brandy if she promised to drink it. Clearly unfamiliar with what passed for a sense of humour among certain undergraduates, Ann agreed and held her hand out for the glass. What he gave her was a huge teapot, brimming with spirits.

Ann made a good fist of it; Harriet helped her out, but it was reckoned that she must have knocked back at least a pint of brandy. She then asked for wine again, but the students denied having any and the two women wandered away. Radcliffe said goodnight to his host and headed back to his rooms, happily unaware that he had just waved goodbye to a promising University career and stepped into one of the nastiest scandals to rock the college in a long while.

It was Joseph Hedges, a porter at St Mary's Hall, who found Ann Crotchley lying in Blue Boar Lane with her head on his door sill and her feet in the gutter, so drunk that she was barely conscious and certainly unable to speak. Fortunately he had his servant boy, James Champ, with him, so the two of them lifted her into the passage beside Hedges' house and Champ stayed with her while Hedges went to find the local watchman. Just down the road he chanced upon Harriet, who told him that Ann was a friend of hers and that she'd see her home. Returning to the drunken woman, they found the watchman of All Saints', Field, had already stumbled over her, and he and a local painter, John Williams, were discussing how to proceed.

There was no question of Harriet seeing her home; Ann was too drunk

Rowlandson's classic engraving of undergraduates sneaking a woman into college while a proctor watches from the shadows.

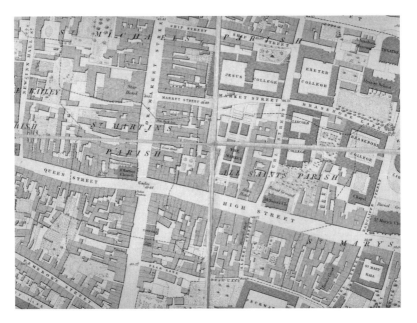

Hoggar's map of Oxford showing the scene of the crime – Brasenose, the High Street, and Blue Boar Lane (here confusingly shown by its alternative name of Bear Lane).

to stand, and the only way she was going to get home was in a barrow. It was suggested to Field that he could put her in his watch box until she sobered up, but he replied, 'I'll see her damned first.' Hedges reckoned it wasn't his problem and vanished into his own house and out of the story. Harriet offered to fetch Ann's landlord to help, but on her way there collapsed in a drunken stupor in New Inn Hall Street, and when she woke up couldn't remember what she was on her way to do. That left Field and Williams with the problem, at which point events took a sinister turn.

There was no suggestion that Ann was anything but drunk. None of the people who'd seen her thought she had any other injury, and various other individuals who passed by – Blue Boar Lane at midnight seems to have been a little like Waterloo Station in the rush hour – supported them. Even the town waits strolled past playing. Esther Simpson and Maria Burley walked past and said Ann's petticoats were up around her knees and she'd lost her cap, but there was no sign any physical harm had come to her. Yet.

In the far right background is the Brasenose staircase on which Houstonne Radcliffe lived.

Field had other work to do; a watchman was supposed to watch, not babysit drunken women in the backstreets. He continued on his rounds, and Williams said he would stay with the woman until Harriet returned with her landlord – he wasn't to know he could wait for the last trump first. That meant Williams was the only person to be alone with Ann after she'd been seen unharmed, which left him in a very unenviable position.

Field passed the word on to other watchmen, and two of them, Cox and Cromwell, came by to look at her. On Cromwell's first visit Ann was unconscious but otherwise fine; on his second he met Williams about 150 yards from where she lay, and Williams said there was no change. On his third visit, with Cox, he saw a good deal of blood beneath her and on her clothes. They loaded the woman on to a barrow and took her back to her lodgings, then sent for Mr Dickeson, a city surgeon and apothecary, to examine her. Mindful of his calling, Dickeson went round to Ann's lodgings at four in the morning and hammered on the door for twenty minutes until Ann's landlady stuck her head out of an upstairs window and asked him what on earth he wanted. He said he'd come to look at the woman who'd been brought home ill, whereupon the landlady said there was no need; Ann Crotchley was just drunk, and it would have been an odd evening when she wasn't brought home in that condition.

As a result, it wasn't until eight that morning that Dickeson got to examine Ann, by which time it was too late. She was unconscious through loss of blood, but Dickeson, who doesn't seem to have been the brightest medical practitioner in Oxford, could see no wound and couldn't work out how this was happening. She grew steadily worse, and died at two the following morning.

Seeing her dilated pupils, and knowing that she had severe stomach pains, Dickeson suspected she might have been poisoned. How exactly this tied up with loss of blood he never explained, but it did mean that he conducted an autopsy, and that was when everything became clear. There was no indication whatsoever of any poison, but a very good reason for loss of blood; someone had driven a sharpened stake up into Ann in a way which, as *Jackson's Oxford Journal* put it, 'we abstain from entering into from motives of delicacy'. She had sustained two major internal wounds and had haemorrhaged to death.

There was no plausible motive for the crime but sheer malice, and only one person who was known to have been alone with her for long enough to carry it out. Williams suddenly found himself the centre of a major investigation.

The authorities' problem was that Williams didn't look much like a murderer. In front of witnesses he'd offered Field a shilling to carry the woman home, and not many murderers are prepared to pay to be deprived of their intended victim. He answered all questions put to him openly, and they had to admit he didn't look like a guilty man; nevertheless, he was all they'd got, so they homed in on him.

Meanwhile all Oxford was buzzing with the case. A reward of £200 had been offered for information leading to capture of the offender, and Harriet Mitchell was happily telling everyone about their encounter at the window of Brasenose. It was hardly possible that Radcliffe had managed to sneak out of college to murder the woman he'd made drunk, but on the other hand if she hadn't been paralytic she might have been able to defend herself. Besides, everyone liked the chance to throw mud at the University. The college authorities may have had a quiet word with the editor of *Jackson's Oxford Journal*; at any rate, a paragraph was inserted to clarify certain matters:

The Sun and other London papers have stated that the girls were called to the room window of a gentleman at Brasenose college, and made to drink; the fact is quite the reverse; they knocked at the window and asked for liquor, which the young men, it may be said imprudently, gave them.

Houstonne Radcliffe quietly left the college about the time of Ann's death, and went home to Limehouse, a college living, where his father was rector.

Meanwhile Williams was committed to gaol to appear before the authorities for further examination. Ann's body, already buried on 12 December with a note in the St Thomas' parish register 'found barbarously murdered in Blue Boor Lane', was dug up again, just to make sure that her death wasn't really due to excess alcohol. There was no doubt; it was murder with a sharp stick, and Williams was brought before the magistrates.

Unfortunately for them, they could find no one who would give Williams the murder weapon. Neither James Champ nor Field the watchman saw Williams with any kind of stick. In fact, the only person in the vicinity who had a stick was Field himself, which rather confused matters. Cromwell then gave Williams further help by swearing that when they met 150 yards from Ann's unconscious form it wasn't on Blue Boar Lane at all but on the High Street, which runs parallel to the lane – in other words, Williams had walked down one of the connecting alleys and away, leaving Ann unguarded. Anyone could have attacked her in his absence.

On the other hand, the original inquest jury had joined the prosecution. Henry Bell, one of the jurors, had decided that if Williams had committed the murder his clothing should be stained with blood. He had the great advantage here that his mother did Williams' washing for him, so he dashed round to see her and demanded to see Williams' shirts. One of them was stained red at the cuff, so he told his mother not to wash it as it would be needed for evidence. She told him not to be stupid; Williams was a painter and his cuff was often stained with red paint. He wrested the shirt from her, and produced it with a flourish in court, where it was agreed the stains looked very much like red paint. He was asked why he had hesitated before showing it to the magistrates.

I did not wish to hurt the feelings of Mr Williams's family.
Had you no other motive?
Not as I know of.

What! Did you not, then, hear of the reward?
Yes, I did. (In a tone of displeasure.)
And that had no effect upon you? (No answer.)

Having disposed of Bell, the magistrates were overwhelmed with contradictory evidence about the stain. A barmaid who saw it at close quarters swore it was paint. Another thought it was blood, but said Williams had been in a scuffle with two gentlemen and had bloodied the nose of one; that was clearly where it came from. A Mrs Barton said Williams had a weak wrist since spraining it and she often bound it for him with an old red watch ribbon which leaked its colour. No one was prepared to accept for a moment that Williams might be guilty. Eventually he was freed without a stain on his character, despite the one on his cuff.

No one was ever convicted of Ann's murder, and the case gradually faded out of the public memory. But one man paid the price for it. When the next University term came round, Houstonne Radcliffe was not to be found in Brasenose. A College Meeting on 31 January 1828 decided: 'H J Radcliffe, having admitted that he gave to Ann Crutchley on the evening of the 5th of December last intoxicating liquor from one of the Windows of this College: Resolved that being now absent he be not allowed to return till after the Long Vacation.'

In fact he never did return. His name remained on the college books, but he was never seen in Oxford again. Humiliation at the scandal?, some wondered. Possibly, but in October 1829 the college authorities received word of a more pressing reason. Houstonne Radcliffe was dead. Ann Crutchley's murderer had claimed a second victim.

The entry for Anne Crotchley's burial in the register of St Thomas's parish – barbarously murdered!

CHAPTER 25

Fireraiser – Spring Heeled Jack v the Robinsons 1861

Arson was a capital crime as far back as the Saxons; even in the nineteenth century it still carried the death penalty. The reason was simple: even if committed with no intent to take human life, fire is such an unpredictable phenomenon that it generally catches the unsuspecting and slow before anyone can prevent it. In 1861 the penalty was reduced to life imprisonment, and by an odd coincidence it was in that year that the most spectacular outbreak of arson Oxfordshire has ever known took place – spectacular not only because of the number of outbreaks, but because they were all in exactly the same place....

The place was Glebe Farm, Fringford, very little of which beyond the living quarters can still have been standing when it was all over. The first fire, on 22 April, destroyed the farm buildings, a corn rick and sundry implements. The second, on 7 July, burned down a round rick of hay in the yard, and the third, *three hours later*, finished off the square rick of hay four yards from it. Two remaining hay ricks were picked off on 23 July. All of which must have been very distressing for the farm's owner, Henry Jerome Augustus Fane de Sallis, Rector of Fringford, but to the exasperation of the police he seemed to be doing everything in his power to protect the culprits.

De Sallis had nothing to do with the farm himself; he leased it out to William Robinson and his wife Mary, and lived himself at the Rectory in the middle of the village a mile and a half away. Nevertheless he was not entirely happy about watching his property burn to the ground, and he called in the County Police to investigate. The police took it seriously; there had been a number of serious fires around Bicester and

Dorchester in which arson was suspected, and this time they were determined to catch the culprit.

According to the Rector, Robinson had worked hard to combat the first fire, saving all the livestock, and his landlord rewarded him with a sovereign. Not to worry, he told the tenant, at least the farm is well insured and no one will be out of pocket. In retrospect this might not have been the wisest course of action. On 7 July Constable James Stone arrived to investigate the round rick fire and found at about quarter to nine in the evening that it was completely extinguished. He could swear to this because, with a singular lack of care for personal comfort, he had thrust his arm deep into the remains of the rick to see if anything was still burning in there. While he was there, he heard de Sallis tell Robinson to keep an eye on things and make sure the fire didn't break out again.

The Reverend Henry Jerome Augustus Fane de Sallis, rector of Fringford, whose part in the Glebe Farm arson was never fully investigated.

Mary Robinson came out into the yard while de Sallis was there and said she wanted to go away. Her husband tried to soothe her, but she insisted she wanted to leave and return to Fringford itself. The police found this suspicious – though many people living on a lonely farm targeted by an arsonist might have felt the same way – but not as suspicious as what

The sketch plan of Glebe Farm included in the prosecution papers for the Robinsons.

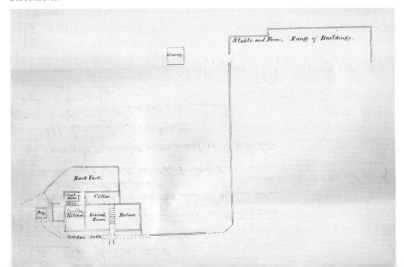

followed. Stone announced his intention of leaving, as everything was under control, but Robinson invited him to stay a little longer and have some of his fresh beer. 'No thanks, I want to go', said Stone, but Robinson and his wife steered him into the house and poured out the drink. As he was sinking the pint, Robinson suddenly said, 'I've left my coat out there – I must go and fetch it', and vanished out into the rick yard, followed by Mary a couple of minutes later.

Stone stayed drinking with Mansfield, the carter, until Robinson returned five minutes later and said everything was all right out in the yard; then he got to his feet to leave but Robinson immediately poured him more beer. He drank this one standing to give himself the chance to leave, when Mary came running into the kitchen from the yard. Stone reckoned it wasn't more than a minute after she came in that he walked out into the yard – to see the square rick blazing away merrily. On the side furthest away from the smouldering remains of the round rick.

The burning rick threw a light like a beacon around the yard and the surrounding fields. Stone quickly scanned the whole area for signs of the arsonist running away, but there was nothing. Behind him, Robinson came out into the yard and said, 'Well this is a pretty job again!', but Stone wasn't paying much attention – he was thinking that the rick must have been burning for at least four minutes when he saw it. Mary Robinson could hardly have failed to notice a huge fire in the yard when she came into the kitchen. Why hadn't she mentioned it?

He and Robinson conducted a search of the area, but Stone didn't expect to find anything. He already had a pretty definite view about who set the rick alight. At eleven that night he was still in the yard when he saw Mary again. She came running in and said she'd been in the Coffee Shop (meaning the privy – there's one euphemism that hasn't made it to the present day) and some man had come running by; she looked out and saw him go through the gate into the field. Stone went to look but saw nothing; he asked the men who were still fetching water to douse the rick fire, but none of them had seen a running man. Going back into the kitchen, he found Mary in her nightgown. She looked at him and said, 'I have no business here. I ought to be at Fringford, and I told our master so.' Slowly Stone was beginning to see how this fitted together.

The police went to see de Sallis and told him of their suspicions – his own tenants were setting light to the farm. De Sallis laughed in their faces. Rubbish, he said, they're good people. You're completely mistaken. The police brought a detective up from London who went over all the evidence and came to the conclusion that the fires must have been set by someone in the farmhouse. De Sallis dismissed the very idea, and the police left, grinding their teeth.

Then the fourth fire broke out. That was bad enough, but it was followed by acts of deliberate vandalism. A harness hanging in the stable was slashed to shreds. Crops were pulled up. The beehive in the garden was overturned. Robinson told de Sallis that he and his wife had been in bed on the night of the beehive incident; he heard the click of the garden gate and the sound of footsteps, but when he looked out of the window he could see nothing and went back to bed. But one thing stuck out like a sore thumb to the police. On the morning after the fire, Stone encountered William Robinson moving the harness about in the stable. On seeing the constable, he said, 'Ah! They've burned all now they could burn, and the next thing that happens will be the harness cut to pieces.' The following day, Stone said darkly, 'You prophesied correctly when you were in the stable', and Robinson replied coolly, 'Yes, I did.'

The police were furious. They demanded that de Sallis co-operate with them in catching the Robinsons red-handed, and to do this they infiltrated one of their own men on to the farm. Henry Toovey, a new constable (and thus unknown) joined the Glebe Farm staff as a carter, with instructions to keep his eyes open.

But nothing happened. The arson attacks absolutely ceased. 'And this is not much to be wondered at,' snarled the police, 'because the Reverend de Sallis had told the Robinsons, and cautioned them that they were suspected and their proceedings were watched.' Still, it was evident that the constabulary were treading on the Robinsons' heels, and by an astonishing coincidence it was just then that the anonymous letters started.

The first was found in the cart hovel by George Pollard, one of the employees, lying on the ground. It read simply:

Don't blame your foreman no longer, for he is innocent as a child unborn. For I done the deed, and my name is Springheel Jack – catch me if you can. But don't blame him no more for you do the wrong man, I am sure. I don't fear none of your police finding me out – you see that.

Spring Heeled Jack was the great bogeyman of the nineteenth century, a mystery which remains unsolved. He was first sighted in 1837 by a businessman returning home in London, who saw a tall, thin figure in a black cloak leap over the railings of a cemetery. The railings were ten feet high, but the figure cleared them with no effort. This worried the businessman rather less than the figure's glowing red eyes and the blue and white flame he spat out of his mouth. The authorities were writing the sighting off as the result of alcoholic indulgence when a figure of exactly the same description attacked a group of four people, ripping the blouse off one Polly Adams and leaving her unconscious. His next appearance was on Clapham Common, and shortly afterwards he landed in front of a coach, sending it out of control and forcing it to crash. Witnesses claimed he escaped by leaping over a nine-foot wall. By 1838 the Lord Mayor of London was describing him as 'a public menace'.

The penny dreadfuls could hardly resist a figure like this, and by the 1860s the name Spring Heeled Jack was as familiar as Batman to a modern audience. Who better to blame for arson attacks than a creature who could spit flame? It was very obliging of the perpetrator to own up and proclaim the innocence of the chief suspects, and the police didn't believe it for a moment. The next day Mary Robinson said to Toovey, 'You see it was not we who did it – the man's name that did do it is Springheel Jack.' Her husband, sitting by the fire, said, 'I should just like to catch Mr Springheel Jack', and Toovey replied feelingly, 'So should I!'

The second letter was found by Harriet Freeman on the potato piece. This one read:

Don't blame William Robinson, for I will say that for him, I do believe he is the honest man in all your lot, for I do think as he had sooner give you anything than harm you. You all blame the wrong man I am sure.

Toovey was hot on the detective trail. He was sneaking round the farmhouse, collecting examples of the handwriting of everyone there, and of the types of paper available in the house – Arthur Conan Doyle would have been proud of him. He found pretty well identical paper to the notes in a pocket book, and reckoned that the handwriting was pretty close to that of Charles Robinson, the couple's son, though he never managed to make this stick in court. Meanwhile more vegetables were pulled up at the farm. Toovey kept watch and saw Mary Robinson in the garden in slippers and shawl, but he never managed to catch her actually pulling anything up. He did find a couple of footprints which he pointed out to her, but she replied, 'It must have been them buggers the police themselves.' The words were reported back by Toovey and didn't help the case, as Mary pointed out she wasn't in the habit of swearing and the phrase was completely implausible for her.

Nevertheless, the police reckoned they'd got enough to go on, and they persuaded de Sallis to bring a prosecution. Yet too many details didn't seem to make sense. When Toovey stood up in court to give his evidence, Mary Robinson fainted at hearing he was a police officer. But the police themselves claimed that de Sallis had tipped the Robinsons off, which is why there were no more arson attacks. Was she just a good actress? She certainly fooled the court if so. More seriously, what was the motive? If Mary was desperate to get back to Fringford, there were simpler ways than burning down the

The village of Fringford, half a century on from the arson attacks.

farm. If her husband was against moving back, why did he appear to be aiding and abetting her? For all the circumstantial evidence against them, the couple were acquitted at the assizes.

The police were not happy with de Sallis; they felt his kindly attitude and refusal to think ill of anyone had cost them the case. No one ever seemed to turn the whole business round and look at it from a different angle. There was one scrap of evidence from George Pollard which never turned up on the formal depositions:

On one Sunday about the latter end of July, William Robinson asked me if I knew what Master had got per bushel for the mustard seed which had been destroyed by the fire. I answered, 'No. Perhaps nine or ten shillings.' Robinson then said he had got fourteen shillings. 'It would have been a damned good job if it had all been burnt,' he said. I replied, 'I think you be a fool.'

Not that big a fool perhaps. The only man who profited from the arson was de Sallis himself, insured up to the hilt by his own admission, and singularly unwilling to prosecute the obvious culprits. A century and a half on, we'll never know – but it is instructive that throughout one of their biggest detective operations to date, the police never even considered the possibility that a gentleman could be a criminal.

CHAPTER 26

A State of Emergency – The Otmoor Riots
1801–32

The Black Death had its advantages. Cutting a swathe through the population of England, it ensured that for several hundred years the amount of land available in the country was adequate to support those who lived on it. Such a state of affairs could not last for ever, and by the nineteenth century agriculture was in difficulties. The old style of farming, with fields cut up into tiny strips and partitioned out around the villagers, could no longer provide enough produce to feed everyone. More intensive farming methods were needed, and for that fields had to be consolidated into blocks and run as a single unit. It was in the nature of things that this change would benefit the wealthy and drive many of the poor into destitution.

In March 1801 the Duke of Marlborough petitioned Parliament for the enclosure of Otmoor in Oxfordshire; the drainage and allotment of 4,000 acres of moorland. This came as a bit of a shock to the inhabitants of the villages on the moor; as far as they were concerned no lord had any absolute rights over it. It didn't fall within anyone's manor. All the villagers were in the habit of using it as and when they wished, and they didn't take kindly to Marlborough's idea of depriving them, which they regarded as something very like theft.

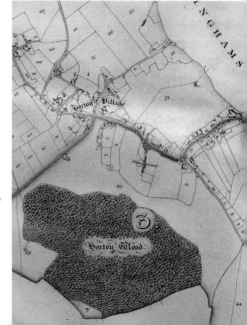

Some of the enclosures which so incensed the inhabitants of Otmoor.

The law locks up the man or woman
Who steals the goose from off the common;
But lets the greater villain loose
Who steals the common from the goose.

When the Parliamentary commissioners tried to affix notices on the church doors at Charlton, Beckley and Oddington announcing the enclosure, they were met by hostile mobs and driven off. Marlborough decided to let it lie, but the idea was revived in 1814 and an enclosure act for Otmoor became law in 1815, despite a petition from four of the Otmoor villages. Drainage was put in hand immediately, and it was this which sunk the poor villagers – any rights they might have to a share in the land when it was divided out were dependent on paying towards the expenses incurred, which of course none of them could afford. A new underclass was instantly created, and one which nursed a burning hatred for the four men seen to be responsible – Sir Alexander Croke, J Sawyer, the Reverend Philip Serle of Oddington, and the Reverend T L Cooke of Beckley.

But enclosure was not a success. In order to keep the water from flooding back onto the moor, absurdly high embankments had been created; this saved the moor all right, but in the wet summer of 1829 ensured that all the other farmland round about was flooded by Otmoor's water. The dispossessed villagers sneaked out by night and dug holes in the embankments, letting the water back. Some of them were taken to court, but the Assizes ruled that there was no case to answer: the enclosure commissioners had no business building embankments that high. In the minds of the villagers this was translated into an official opinion that the enclosure had been illegal – and that was when the trouble started in earnest.

Captain Swing had nothing on the Otmoor Rioters. A systematic campaign of violence and destruction got under way, with fences smashed and buildings torn down. The magistrates of Oxfordshire held an emergency meeting, and agreed to 'sanction such extraordinary measures and expenses as shall appear expedient'. Put simply, they knew the extent of the violence was beyond them: 'it is the unanimous conviction of this court that the strongest constabulary force which the magistrates of the county have it within their means to raise for the suppression of the outrages will prove totally powerless and insufficient'. It wasn't as if they could even trust their Special Constables: 'they would be remiss if not altogether unwilling to do their duty, not only from a fear to resist such a force as the assembled rioters would present, but also from their entire concurrence with the views and purposes of the rioters themselves'. The enemy was inside the gates.

The magistrates decided they had to fight violence with violence. They voted to ask for a force of armed police officers to be sent down from London, and for the Oxfordshire Yeomanry to be called out. When the fourteen policemen arrived, it was decided to station them where most of the disturbances had taken place, and the villagers of Charlton were asked to lodge them. This suggestion was met with hysterical laughter on the part of the villagers, on the obvious if unstated grounds that you don't billet an army on the enemy.

Meanwhile a handful of the rioters had been summoned to court for trespass; Kirby and Price, two of them, were heard saying that no one would dare appear against them and the magistrates were just trying to bankrupt them with legal expenses. Sensing a possible means of negotiation with the rioters, the magistrates sent a policeman in to make them a proposal, but they beat him up severely and threw him back at his employers. The magistrates then asked Sergeant Chamberlayne who led the police force if he felt he would be able to deal with any outbreaks of violence, to which Chamberlayne rather acidly replied that if a couple of hundred

The Oxfordshire Yeomanry, looking better than when the mob had finished with them.

rioters attacked fourteen policemen the outcome was a foregone conclusion. The police were already armed with a staff and cutlass each, but considering this the magistrates bought each of them a pistol as well.

The whole thing looks like a huge overreaction on the part of the authorities, but was in fact a reaction to the most notorious incident of the Otmoor riots, and one which hadn't happened anywhere near Otmoor at all.

During 1830, before the coming of the armed police, gangs of hundreds of people appeared on the moor on moonlit nights, armed with billhooks, hacking down hedges and wrecking bridges. As time went on the mobs became bolder, until they were seen out in broad daylight, openly defying the forces of law and order. By early September the owners of the enclosures on Otmoor were looking at the complete destruction of their property, and complained loudly to the county magistrates, asking what exactly the local yeomanry were for. The Oxfordshire and Bucks Yeomanry were duly called out and the magistrates themselves held a meeting at Islip on 6 September, where they were told that a mob of about 500 people were destroying the enclosures only a mile away.

This was a little difficult to ignore, so the High Sheriff and Joseph Henley rode out onto the moor, making sure the Yeomanry were just behind them, and asked the leaders of the mob what they thought they were doing. 'Otmoor for ever!' cried the mob. We're happy to talk to a delegation of your leaders, the magistrates said. 'Otmoor for ever!' yelled the mob. Are there any churchwardens or overseers of the poor among you, asked the magistrates. 'Otmoor for ever!' screamed the mob. Tiring of this one-sided conversation, the magistrates read the riot act and called the Yeomanry in.

The military succeeded in arresting some sixty or seventy of the rioters without any great violence taking place, and escorted them to Islip, where they were charged with riotous behaviour by the Reverend Vaughan Thomas – possibly the most active magistrate of the era and no friend to the poorer classes who didn't know their place – and forty-two of them committed to Oxford Gaol. They were placed in two wagons and, under the guard of the Yeomanry commanded by Captain Hamilton,

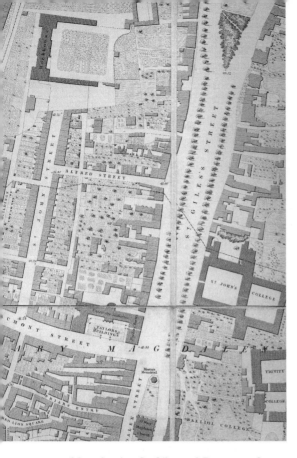

taken the seven miles into Oxford. This was a serious mistake.

Any other day of the year, there might have been no problem. Any other route into Oxford might have been clear. But they were coming from the north, which meant they had to enter the broad thoroughfare of St Giles, leading past St John's College. And 6 September was the Monday after St Giles' Day, which meant St Giles Fair.

The Fair had evolved out of the old St Giles parish wake. By the nineteenth century it was a riot of booths, salesmen, rides,

Map showing St Giles and Beaumont Street, where the crowd freed the Otmoor rioters.

attractions, freak shows – then, as today, it effectively closed down the whole street for its duration. And Hamilton proposed to escort two wagons full of prisoners straight through the middle of it.

'It is hardly necessary to say', the magistrates observed when it was all over, 'that this fair was not comprised of the haut ton of Oxford.' Even the better class of people who visited the fair

St Giles Fair in the 1860s, thirty years after the yeomanry were attacked there.

Beaumont Street, being constructed in the 1820s.

tended to let their hair down there, and most of the people on the street that evening had no love for the Yeomanry. When they discovered who the Yeomanry were escorting, all hell broke loose.

The news ran like wildfire through the crowd, many of whom had strong sympathies with the rioters, and cries of abuse filled the air. Then some of the crowd scooped gravel and dirt up off the roadway and threw it at the soldiers. The wagons were surrounded by people yelling 'Otmoor for ever!' and 'Damned if you shall ever go to gaol! We will release you presently!' Hamilton kept a stony face, leading his troops the endless quarter mile down to the junction with Beaumont Street where he could turn off towards Oxford Castle. Just as he reached it, the pent-up violence of the crowd broke out.

A hail of stones and sticks was flung at the militia. William Bartley, a sergeant major, was struck by bricks, which knocked his cap flying, then struck his head, sending him off his horse with blood streaming into his eyes. He crashed to the ground and had to be carried away by his colleagues, spending the next two months under the care of three surgeons. Around him, fellow members of the Yeomanry were flinging up their hands to ward off the missiles. Cries of 'Go it, my boys! Unhorse the buggers!' could be heard. Charles Tomes, one of the Yeomanry, saw John Sydenham with an odd sort of stick in his hand – the kind used in one of the fairground booths for throwing at snuff boxes in an attempt to win them – but only noticed this in passing as he turned to protect himself from an assailant; then he felt a terrific blow as the stick broke across the back of his head.

While part of the crowd beat down the mounted escort, others worked at releasing the prisoners. Thomas Davies saw an old acquaintance of his, William Price, calling to the prisoners, 'Jump over, my boys, and we will assist you!' He called to Price, 'You ought to know better', to which Price replied, 'Damn your eyes, you ought to be drowned!' The prisoners were scrambling over the tailboards of the wagons, helped by the mob, but one sergeant, John Quarterman, fought back to hang on to the worst of the Otmoor rioters, a man called Gibbard who had been charged with malicious wounding. The crowd closed in on him and beat him so badly that he was unable to move his limbs; Gibbard meanwhile ran for it.

None of the prisoners ever reached the gaol. They vanished among the booths and sideshows of the fair, while the Yeomanry fought their way out to safety. Attempts to prosecute the mob were largely unsuccessful – the victims were unable to recognize their assailants, and in the end only Sydenham and William Collins were brought to court and found guilty. They got a trivial sentence of two months each. The magistrates may have been exaggerating when they suggested that the mob was comprised of the lower elements of society; although the two scapegoats were labourers, several gentlemen were named as being involved in the attack.

In the wake of the St Giles incident, tensions out on the moor were bound to be high. But this was a typical example of guerrilla warfare. As long as armed police were in evidence, there were no incidents; once the police presence was reduced to save money, the disturbances started again. After a period of calm in 1832 much of the force was stood down; promptly a mob appeared and destroyed a bridge and a mile and a half of fences.

Meanwhile the police were in confusion. Proprietors of land on Otmoor who attempted to replace their fences had them broken down again. A certain Higgs of Murcott pounded some cattle, but the mob released them again and beat him up before they left. Windows were broken in the houses where the police were lodged. Five of the constables laid charges of inefficiency and poor conduct against Sergeant

Chamberlayne, but when the magistrates investigated it turned out that the charges had actually been drawn up on their behalf by one of the more notorious Otmoor rioters. Nevertheless, Chamberlayne resigned, and under his successor Layard things began to improve.

Simply, the Otmoor disturbances could not go on much longer. The cottagers who made up the mobs had to eat; they couldn't go on fighting against circumstances for ever with no hope of change. They could do damage to the property of those who had taken away their livelihood, but the police were on the side of the property owners, and the enclosures would never be reversed. Gradually they fell away, either finding a new way of living with the situation or moving to become part of the slow drift of the labouring poor into the towns.

But the authorities had learned one thing. Popular resentment was now a force to be reckoned with, and sending in the Yeomanry was far from a guarantee of restoring order. The property owners were no longer going to get everything their own way – and any attempt to do so was likely to lead to more bloodshed in the streets. The lesson was learned quickly – in England, bloodbaths tend to be the province of criminals, not revolutionaries.

CHAPTER 27

Epilogue – The Ones that Got Away

Many of the foul deeds and suspicious deaths of Oxfordshire are hinted at only in passing. For every instance where we have something like the full story, there are a dozen in which an odd line or comment suggests something which would be worth investigating if the evidence survived.

Oxfordshire Record Office is full of such tantalizing snippets. As far back as 1300, at the time of the baby-eating pig, the coroner's roll indicates a town where one had to be very careful to survive in one piece:

John Metescarp, found dead in the house of Ralph le Cyrgion in Oxford St Aldates, wounded with an arrow. Michael, Manciple of Bole Hall, is accused of his murder.

William de Neusham died in Oxford St Martin. He and other servants of John de Lytegrene had seen John Beneyt junior urinating between two stalls. Neusham drew his sword and struck John, who ran to the house of John Beneyt senior. The two of them re-emerged with John de Walteford, and in the ensuing brawl William was killed by John junior.

William de Heyworth of St Cross Holywell died after being struck on the head with a hatchet by Reginald le Messer one evening.

Margery of Hereford died in a house in St Aldates Oxford after one Richard (whose surname is not known) had one evening gone to bed with her, and then stabbed her by her left breast.

Henry de Bokingham was found dead in the parish of Oxford St Mary the Virgin. He had gone to the crossroads called la Wytecrouch and had been killed by unknown robbers.

Robert de Honyton, clerk, died in the parish of Oxford St Michael at the Northgate. He had climbed the belltower of the church to ring the bells, but fell out through a door on to the ground. He died a few days later.

Not that such violence was confined to the mediaeval period. Sometimes the high jinks of students could get out of hand. In Brasenose College on 5 November 1890, the students lit a huge bonfire in the quad but realized that it seemed to be lacking something without a guy. They kidnapped Chandler, the Vice Principal, and threw him on the fire; the porters trying to rescue him were beaten back, and only by bringing in reinforcements from among the scouts did they manage to haul him off the pyre and back to his rooms. Some years later F W Bussell,

The old quad of Brasenose College, where the Vice-Principal ended up standing in for Guy Fawkes on a bonfire.

the college dandy, made a point of never walking through the quad on 5 November, having a sneaking suspicion that he was exactly the type of figure to be next in line for the flames.

It's not only documentary evidence which gives us these glimpses of dubious goings-on in past centuries. Sometimes the bodies themselves resurface. During the building of Beaumont Street in the 1820s a pit full of skeletons emerged, while recent excavations around Oxford Castle for the redevelopment of the site discovered a number of human remains cut about in very odd ways – suggesting that some underhand anatomizing may have been going on quietly behind the scenes on executed criminals.

This is only what one would expect from a city whose patron saint is St Frideswide. The daughter of a Saxon nobleman, sought in marriage by a pagan Mercian king, she refused to submit and fled to the woods where she lived with swineherds for several years. Furious, the Mercian king marched on Oxford with his troops, but when he arrived there a sudden burst of lightning struck him blind.

He should have been grateful it was no worse.

The shrine of St Frideswide in Christ Church Cathedral.

Index